Disruptive Procurement

Michael F. Strohmer • Stephen Easton • Martin Eisenhut
Elouise Epstein • Robert Kromoser • Erik R. Peterson
Enrico Rizzon

Disruptive Procurement

Winning in a Digital World

KEARNEY

🐎 Springer

Michael F. Strohmer
Kearney
Vienna, Austria

Martin Eisenhut
Kearney
Munich, Germany

Robert Kromoser
Kearney
Vienna, Austria

Enrico Rizzon
Kearney
Melbourne, VIC, Australia

Stephen Easton
London, UK

Elouise Epstein
Kearney
San Francisco, VA, USA

Erik R. Peterson
Kearney's Global Business Policy Council
Arlington, VA, USA

ISBN 978-3-030-38949-9   ISBN 978-3-030-38950-5 (eBook)
https://doi.org/10.1007/978-3-030-38950-5

This Springer imprint is published by the registered company Springer Nature Switzerland AG
The registered company address is: Gewerbestrasse 11, 6330 Cham, Switzerland

Preface

Disruption and digital. These two words seem to be the two most used words in our environment right now. Everybody is talking about disruption and digital and is attracted to these words. But it seems there is no common understanding about what they really mean and how these two forces are influencing – and shaping – the global economy and all industries. While it would take an encyclopedia to provide insights about the impact of disruption and digital for every industry and every region, we are taking a humbler approach here and covering the impact and conclusions for procurement.

In procurement, disruption is waiting in the wings; executives see and feel it coming and have glimpsed the impact, but its full force has not yet been unleashed. This means now is the time to create and implement your vision for the future of procurement.

We at Kearney see disruption in procurement in different ways and discuss it in multiple contexts throughout this book. We start with a sensibilization of disruption and the global trends behind it in ▶ Chapter 1 and outline the future of procurement in ▶ Chapter 2.

In ▶ Chapter 3, we show how new technologies and capabilities are leading to whole new (disruptive) ways of working in procurement and how digitalization is simplifying operational procurement while – much more importantly – it is enabling strategic procurement to go new ways.

This is the main focus of ▶ Chapter 4, as well. Here, we talk about disruption as a result of laying a strong foundation in procurement by linking the value chain to the customer view. With these building blocks in place, procurement has the capacity to make full use of the data, knowledge, and insight it has in its treasure troves. It can use these resources to help the business grow, find new sources of innovation, and reduce multiple types of risk.

Looking forward, we expect, as described in ▶ Chapter 5, that the face of procurement will change as it gains the capacities and skills to manage larger and more complex value chain processes. Similarly, we see that procurement will become the central data hub of the enterprise – a place that uses its knowledge to pursue growth through innovation in product and services, as well as the identification of external innovation.

No matter how disruption manifests itself, we believe that procurement is getting smarter, smaller, and speedier and needs to grow into a new role as a big-thinking, proactive, integrated, and service-oriented innovation scout for the enterprise.

That's a tall order, we realize. But if procurement does not rise to the challenge of reinventing itself in these ways, it will cease to exist as we know it. Already, with the introduction of robotic process automation, we expect operational procurement to be radically different within the next few years.

With this as a backdrop, we at Kearney felt it's time to pull together in book form a discussion of the trends that are reshaping procurement fast and furiously.

We also found this the right opportunity to introduce a new framework, which we are calling Disruptive Procurement, in which procurement itself is a disruptor.

In 2008, Kearney launched *The Purchasing Chessboard: 64 Methods to Reduce Costs and Increase Value with Suppliers* – introducing methods and levers for state-of-the-art category management. The objective in this framework is to achieve the highest possible sustainable savings and generate value by applying one of the 64 levers we defined.

In 2012, Kearney launched *The CPO: Transforming Procurement in the Real World*, which has helped hundreds of clients holistically transform their organizations by creating higher levels of effectiveness in the function internally and with external suppliers.

In 2014, we published *True SRM*, a completely new way to manage suppliers that supports companies in producing the results wanted by the buyer, such as providing particular innovations. Its objective is to obtain competitive advantage and maximize the value generated with suppliers by applying tailored interaction models. The models should be based on performance and strategic potential.

Now, we are publishing the Disruptive Procurement framework.

Is this just another procurement framework?

Not in our opinion.

The Disruptive Procurement framework can be used to reinvent the way things are done within an industry. It is possible because of deep knowledge of the value creation process at suppliers, as well as knowing the value your own company creates for clients. Typically, Disruptive Procurement is mandated by the CEO.

Through years of project work in procurement, and in hundreds if not thousands of conversations with clients, we have come to believe that the next generation of value creation needs to be based on the complete product and service line of a company. To create value, the resources within procurement's sphere of influence must be used completely. Procurement must take on a role as an impactful networker, helping to make decisions and execute on projects within company functions and with suppliers.

This book is one of our answers to the challenge and question of how to create value in a disrupted and digital business environment.

Many thanks to these colleagues for their contributions:
Sameer Anand, Jonathan C. Anscombe, Johannes C. Aurik, John D. Blascovich, Patrick Van den Bossche, Marina Catino, Nithin Chandra, Laurent Chevreux, Mark R. Clouse, Ana Maria Conde, Imran Dassu, Fred Eng, Kai Engel, John Paul Fiorentino, Colin Glasgow, Jules A. Goffre, Mui-Fong Goh, Paulo Goncalves, Benoit Gougeon, David Gowans, Michael D. Hales, Carlos Higo, Marc Hochman, Robert Harold Holt, Per Kristian Hong, Siddharth Jain, Bharat Kapoor, Arun Kochar, Tomotsugu Kozaki, Remco Kroes, Hitoshi Kuriya, Marc Lakner, Robin Lemke, Brooks A. Levering, Kaushika S. Madhavan, Lynne Ann McDonnel, Steven Mehltretter, Xavier Mesnard, Alberto Oca, Joon Leong Ooi, Jan van der Oord, Jim Pearce, Philip Rauen, Etienne Sebaux, Subramaniam Pazhayanur Shanmukham, Yves Thill, William Roylan Tribe, Badrinath Veeraghanta, Jane Wanklyn, Fwei Keat Yap, Fabio Eiji Yoshitome, and Michael W. Zimmerman.

And a special acknowledgment to other authors of The Purchasing Chessboard: 64 Methods to Reduce Costs and Increase Value with Suppliers: Christian Schuh, Jim Pearce, Alenka Triplat, and Joe Raudabaugh. In addition, thanks to the authors of the initial paper on Disruptive Procurement: Christian Schuh, Alenka Triplat, Harald Jordan, Damon Broder, and Angela Chang.

The following experts in digital procurement provided important insights for this book: Michael Römer, Jens Behre, Paul Mahlke, Enzio Reincke and Charlotte Winkelmayer.

Michael F. Strohmer
Vienna
Austria

Stephen Easton
London
UK

Martin Eisenhut
Munich
Germany

Elouise Epstein
San Francisco
CA, USA

Robert Kromoser
Vienna
Austria

Erik R. Peterson
Arlington
VA, USA

Enrico Rizzon
Melbourne
VIC, Australia

Contents

About the Authors

Michael F. Strohmer

Michael F. Strohmer is a partner who co-leads Kearney's European Strategic Operations Practice. He is one of the founders of PERLab in Europe.

Based in Vienna, Austria, he joined the firm in 2001. He has led projects with a broad range of international clients, mainly in post-merger integration and carve outs. His work encompasses the utilities, automotive, consumer goods, and process industries in various European countries, as well as in Asia and the United States.

He is an expert in operations and procurement transformation, post-merger management, raw materials, and large-scale CAPEX projects. He has published several books and is also coauthor of the books *The Purchasing Chessboard: 64 Methods to Reduce Costs and Increase Value with Suppliers, Supplier Relationship Management: Unlocking the Hidden Value in Your Supply Base*, and *The CPO: Transforming Procurement in the Real World*.

Michael likes to discuss with CxOs the future of the economy and especially the future of operations. He earned doctorate degrees in business administration and in law. He lives in Austria's picturesque lake region near Salzburg.

Stephen Easton

Stephen Easton has two decades of experience working with procurement organizations to help them grow their capabilities and create more value for their businesses.

His work is cross-industry and encompasses sectors as diverse as banking and aerospace. He started his career as a chartered management accountant and holds an MBA from Cornell University. His first degree was in politics, philosophy, and economics from Oxford.

Martin Eisenhut

Martin Eisenhut is a partner and managing director of Kearney's Central Europe unit. Based in Munich, he is also global leader of the firm's Industrial Goods & Services Practice and leader of the Aerospace & Defense Practice for the Europe, Middle East, and Africa region.

Martin has extensive experience as a manufacturing strategy consultant and has supported an array of projects in engineered products, automation, aerospace and defense, automotive supply, and microelectronics.

He is widely recognized as a leader in industrial goods and services and also holds supervisory board positions in Europe.

Before joining Kearney, he was the global head of the Engineered Products and High Tech Competence Center at Roland Berger Strategy Consultants in Munich and was a member of the Supervisory Board.

He earned his computer science degree at the University of Passau in Germany and his doctorate in computer science at the Technical University of Munich. He also completed an apprenticeship as a skilled worker in a machinery company.

Elouise Epstein

Elouise Epstein is a digital procurement futurist and Kearney vice president based in San Francisco.

She has nearly two decades of experience working with procurement and supply chain organizations to architect, design, and adopt digital technologies. She works to disrupt subpar technology adoption and build future strategies through advanced partnerships with startups and emerging technology solution providers.

She is an inaugural member of ISM's Thought Leadership Council and frequent writer and presenter about digital procurement. She is coauthor of Kearney's Future of Procurement whitepapers, a 12-part series developed in partnership with leading clients that charts a vision for future success in procurement.

Robert Kromoser

Robert Kromoser has been with Kearney since 1998. He is based in Vienna, Austria, and gained most of his consulting experience in international projects in Germany, Switzerland, Belgium, Denmark, the Netherlands, France, Italy, Great Britain, Taiwan, and the United States. He is a member of the leadership team of Kearney's Procurement Practice, with a focus on strategic sourcing, procurement transformation, and supplier risk management.

He has led multiple projects in the automotive, construction equipment and machinery, chemicals, and building materials industries.

In several studies, he analyzed the role of strategic sourcing and procurement as a value-adding factor. He is also coauthor of *The Purchasing Chessboard: 64 Methods to Reduce Costs and Increase Value with Suppliers*.

He studied business administration at Vienna University of Economics and Business Administration in Austria and at Carnegie Mellon University in the United States. He lives near Vienna's famous baroque park, Augarten.

Erik R. Peterson

Erik R. Peterson is a partner at Kearney and managing director of the firm's Global Business Policy Council (GBPC), a strategic advisory service for business leaders. In the most recent survey of the University of Pennsylvania's assessment of 6,600 think tanks, the GBPC was ranked the second best for-profit think tank in the world.

Since joining Kearney in 2010, he has guided initiatives relating to strategic foresight, including a program on scenario planning with Oxford University and summits on strategic planning. In 2017, he was elected to the board of Kearney's Energy Transition Institute.

He is also a senior advisor at the Center for Strategic and International Studies (CSIS). Formerly, he was senior vice president at CSIS and held the CSIS William A. Schreyer Chair in Global Analysis. Before joining CSIS, he was Director of Research at Kissinger Associates.

Erik received an MBA from the Wharton School, an MA from The Johns Hopkins University School of Advanced International Studies, and a BA from Colby College.

Enrico Rizzon

Enrico Rizzon is a partner in Kearney's Melbourne office who has a decade of consulting experience primarily focused on organizational productivity and transformation programs.

Recently, his focus has been on procurement and the ever-growing application of analytics in business. He now leads Kearney's Procurement and Analytics Solutions Practice for Asia Pacific.

He speaks regularly at conferences and frequently writes on procurement-driven transformation and more recently on the competitive advantage that can be driven through analytically enabled organizations.

He is chairman of the Melbourne Business School Centre for Business Analytics, where he helps shape future talent and research on business analytics.

He has an undergraduate degree in chemical engineering (Hons) from the University of Adelaide and an MBA from the Melbourne Business School.

Introduction

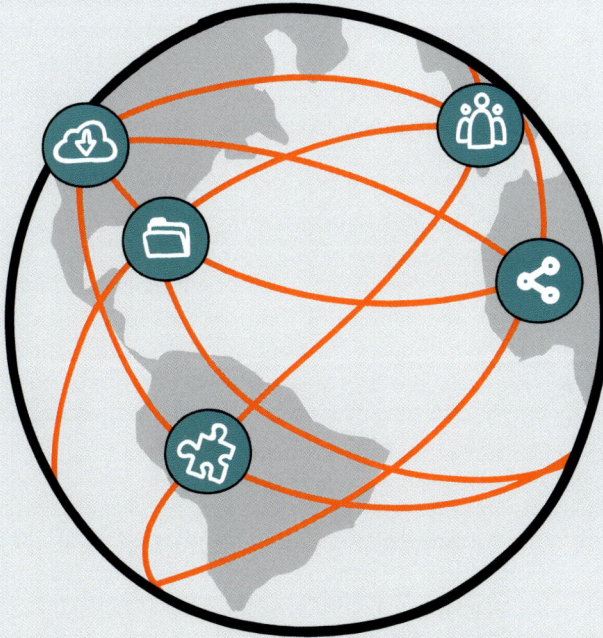

Contents

© Springer Nature Switzerland AG 2020
M. F. Strohmer et al., *Disruptive Procurement*, https://doi.org/10.1007/978-3-030-38950-5_1

1

The Disruptive Setting for Disruptive Procurement

"What if?" That was the simple and elegant title of an opinion piece that *New York Times* columnist Thomas Friedman wrote in January 2013 about circumstances that applied then and continue to apply today. The point of Friedman's essay was to ask whether "the recent turmoil in international markets isn't just the product of tremors but rather of seismic shifts in the foundational pillars of the global system, with highly unpredictable consequences"?[1] In short, he wisely challenged us to consider the proposition that "a bunch of eras are ending all at once."

Our answer to that challenge is categorical: Yes, they are. A bunch of eras are ending all at once.

In light of the significant global uncertainties that have emerged since Friedman's column, spanning geopolitical, macroeconomic, social, and commercial spheres across diverse geographical regions, there can be little doubt that we are indeed in the midst of a "seismic" redefinition of fundamental conditions. There can also be little doubt that the repercussions for the future of globalization, a phenomenon that many of us have come to take for granted, will be profound.

We need to emphasize, however, that this confluence of circumstances, as important as it appears to be, is by no means unique. We saw a similar constellation of seismic changes a decade ago, for example, in the financial turmoil generated by the Great Recession. Similarly, a quarter century ago, we saw the confluence of a number of profound transitions when the end of the Cold War, the sweeping political and economic transition in Eastern Europe, and the transformation of systems in many developing countries ushered in a remarkable period. It was a period that many of us thought and hoped was the immutable reaffirmation of democratization and market-based economic policies.[2]

After the devastation of WWII and the fight against rising fascism, we saw the fundamental transition that was part and parcel of the geopolitical redefinition of the world, from the United Nations system to the Bretton Woods framework for economic ties. We saw a global "rebalancing" in the aftermath of WWI, the consequence of the rise of nationalism and populism, and as a result of the seminal technological advances of the time. Of course, in the vast historical sweep, there are countless other examples we could point to.

Each one of these historical inflection points, and the varying disruptions they have engendered, has challenged the very nature of commerce. They have generated new and unique combinations of opportunities and challenges for business. They have transformed marketplaces in important and differing ways. And they have stepped on the accelerator—or slammed on the brakes—of globalization, and the cross-border movement of goods and services, as well as capital, technology and ideas.

Considering this, the right starting point for the discussion about the changing nature and role of procurement is in recognition that the macro environment within which the procurement story is unfolding, and will continue to unfold, is itself

---

1   Thomas L. Friedman, "What If?" *New York Times*, January 20, 2016.
2   Francis Fukuyama, *The End of History and the Last Man* (New York: Avon Books, 1992).

disruptive. The current prospects suggest that we are moving from a quarter-century of rapid globalization, marked in particular by the stunning rise of China in the global economy, into a phase of heightened nationalism and mercantilism. We therefore want to advance some thoughts here, not on "what if?" but rather "what now?" when it comes to practicing Disruptive Procurement in an increasingly volatile environment.

Anticipating the Next Phase

What, then, will be the disruptive external context for the continued evolution of procurement?

We start with Friedman's proposition that "a bunch of eras may be ending all at once." In our view, the main areas of the ongoing "seismic" redefinition of the marketplace include the changing geopolitical balance, core shifts in economics (across the spectrum, from production to policy), the impact of exponential technologies, eroding institutions and the decay of public trust. Some analysts have dubbed it an "age of insecurity," and indeed, many of the core assumptions, knowledge sets, relationships and institutions that have defined our world over the past 25 years are shifting rapidly.

Each one of these "ending eras" is in itself highly significant. When considered together, however, they signal a wholesale departure from the world of liberalization and globalization that we have known. Similarly, they signal the need for new and ever more innovative approaches to procurement, sourcing strategies, management of global supply chains, and interlinked international operations.

To set the context for our deep dive into Disruptive Procurement, we offer here an examination of each of these forces and their implications for commerce. Because they each generate uncertainties about the outlook for globalization, we also will assess potential future directions for globalization and the general environment for procurement.

Immutable Shifts in the Global Geopolitical Balance

The first of these "ending eras" is the move away from a quarter century of U. S. supremacy and relative geopolitical and economic stability that followed the ignominious collapse of the Soviet Union in 1991. Have we reached *the end of "the end of history,"* the compelling thesis of preeminent democracy and market-based economics advanced by scholar Francis Fukuyama?[3] It certainly looks that way. Under the current circumstances, Fukuyama himself has expressed concern about the rapid erosion of liberal democracy and the weakness of the same established institutions whose legitimacy and sustainability he earlier believed to be incontrovertible. In a recent article, he bemoans the rise of the "very worrisome phenomenon" of populist nationalism.[4]

---

3   Francis Fukuyama, *The End of History and the Last Man* (New York: Avon Books, 1992).
4   Francis Fukuyama, "The rise of populist nationalism," in Credit Suisse Research Institute, *The Future of Politics: 2018 Davos Edition* (Zurich: Credit Suisse: 2018).

1

Great power relations and the shifting balance of power are at the center of the new environment in which leaders worldwide must now maneuver. In place of the earlier "hyper-puissance"[5] order, during which the United States was the uncontested global superpower, what has emerged is a multipolar system in which old rivalries have been renewed, traditional regional contests have reheated, new contests have materialized, and new actors, including non-national players such as the terror group Al Qaeda and ISIS militants, are playing an increasingly important role.

Speaking to the U.S. Senate Armed Services Committee, former U.S. Secretary of State Henry Kissinger recently described the overarching geopolitical shifts in these terms:

> » The international situation facing the United States is unprecedented. What is occurring is more than a coincidence of individual crises across various geographies. Rather, it is a systemic failure of world order which, after gathering momentum for nearly two decades, is trending towards the international system's erosion rather than its consolidation, whether in terms of respect for sovereignty, rejection of territorial acquisition by force, expansion of mutually beneficial trade without geo-economic coercion, or encouragement of human rights. In the absence of a shared concept among the major powers expansive enough to accommodate divergent perspectives of our national interests, partially derived from our diverse historical experiences, traditional patterns of great power rivalry are returning.[6]

The sharp deterioration of relations between Washington and Moscow, punctuated by the escalating debate over Russian interference in the 2016 U.S. presidential elections, is eerily reminiscent of the deep-seated tensions that marked much of the Cold War period. So, too, is the abrupt revival of the strategic arms race and the escalation of proxy conflicts—from Ukraine to Syria—across the planet. It is no exaggeration to assert, as Council on Foreign Relations President Richard N. Haass has, that we have entered a new Cold War.[7] Certainly the recent vitriol from Russia's President Vladimir Putin, in announcing the development of a new generation of "invincible" nuclear missiles, echoed the famous "we will bury you" threat issued by Soviet Premier Nikita Khrushchev some six decades ago.[8]

The rapid political, economic and diplomatic rise of China, of course, is another major factor in the altered geostrategic landscape. In the space of a quarter century, on the basis of an historically unprecedented economic expansion, the country is seeking to strengthen its role both regionally and globally in ways that were nearly inconceivable when the process began.

---

5   The expression was introduced by former U.S. National Security Advisor Zbigniew Brzezinski in 1997, in his seminal book *The Great Chess Board: America and the Rest of the World* (New York: Basic Books, 1997). Brzezinski posited that the United States was the only power to have supremacy in the four key areas: military, economic, technological and cultural. The rubric was later (1999) used by then French foreign minister Hubert Védrine to describe the position of the United States in the post-Cold War world.

6   Henry A. Kissinger, Opening Statement, Senate Armed Services Committee, January 25, 2018.

7   Richard N. Haass, "Cold War II," Project Syndicate, February 23, 2018. Haass argues that a "quarter-century after the end of the Cold War, we unexpectedly find ourselves in a second one."

8   See "Russia's Putin unveils 'invincible' nuclear weapons," *BBC News*, March 1, 2018.

These distinct factors all add up to massive uncertainties. How will the new geo-political balance evolve in a genuinely multipolar world? With U.S.-Russian relations currently under serious pressure, how will they change? Will we see direct conflict and indirect competition through proxy states and actors, due to a new period of structural tensions? How will the rapid rise of China affect the international system and the rules that have governed relations since the end of the WWII? And what are the implications on business of global pandemics, such as the coronavirus?

What happens will define the degree to which there is a secure, stable and prosperous operating environment for companies worldwide. It will foreordain – or determine beforehand – global supply-demand trends, the path of globaliza-tion, the balance between globalism and regionalism, the level and flows of trade and investment, the role of governments in legislation and regulation, and the future shape of markets.

New Macroeconomic Uncertainties

Leaders today must also address profound uncertainties in macroeconomics. In particular, they must answer new questions about our understanding of econom-ics and its core measures, the "return of history" when it comes to monetary policy and cost of capital, a growing public backlash to the paradigm of glo-balization, and persistent questions regarding stratification of wealth, income, opportunity, knowledge and more.

At the core of this challenge facing leaders is the nagging question of whether the "dismal science" of economics has stayed up to speed with the very circum-stances it endeavors to explain. The answer is not clear. Ever since the onset of the Great Recession, which itself came as a surprise to most prominent economists, the field has been characterized by lingering debates over what new approaches and measures should be used to define economic activity.

In fact, ironically, some of the most prominent economists themselves have been the sources of the most virulent criticism. Paul Krugman, the Nobel-laureate who is Distinguished Professor of Economics at the Graduate Center of the City University of New York and columnist for *The New York Times*, argued way back in 2009 that macroeconomics over the previous 30 years was "spectacularly useless at best, and positively harmful at worst."[9] For leaders, this is hardly an academic debate. The capacity of the economics profession to get things right—from deciphering the dynamics to pinpointing the right measures in growth, inflation, productivity, and a number of other economic fundamen-tals—has staggering real-world implications.

Then there is the "return of history"—the gradual return of economic circum-stances that prevailed prior to the Great Recession. In particular, this translates into the end of the period of monetary policies and practices that brought interest

9   Speech before the London School of Economics, Lionel Robbins Lecture, June 10, 2009, as reported in "The Other Worldly Philosophers," *The Economist*, July 16, 2009.

1

rates down to zero (or, in some cases, rates that were negative). The current outlook for the gradual return of higher rates—and its consequences for debt-servicing by a range of countries across the planet—suggests continued uncertainty. So, too, does the potential asymmetry between the policies of the Federal Reserve Bank, the European Central Bank, the Bank of Japan, and other central banks.

Another source of uncertainty, as we will see later in this chapter, is the growing backlash to globalization. As public dissatisfaction with dislocation continues to grow, the corresponding rise of economic nationalism and protectionism is a clear and present danger. At the time of writing, the prospect of additional trade tensions loomed large, and the uncertainties for leaders were multiplying rapidly.

The underlying numbers are sobering. Trade as a share of global growth domestic product (GDP) has still not recovered to the level before the global financial crisis. The share of exports moving through cross-border supply chains has also stagnated at just under 60 percent since 2007, after rising from about 50 percent during the previous decade. These trends are due in part to a rise in protectionist actions. Furthermore, while some notable bilateral trade deals have been completed, the passage of large multilateral trade deals is increasingly rare. The Doha Round of World Trade Organization (WTO) negotiations, first launched in 2001, remains stalled and shows little sign of life. Policy uncertainty remains a top risk. Should more anti-trade measures materialize, the WTO warns, "this proliferation of trade restrictive measures and the uncertainty created by such action could place the economic recovery in jeopardy."[10] In late 2018, the trade impacted by import-restrictive measures was estimated at 588 billion dollars—no less than seven times greater than the previously reported WTO figure.

There are other crucial questions regarding the medium-term global economic outlook that business leaders need to take into account. In particular, as the world's major economies emerge from the low interest rate environment, uncertainties loom large about whether leaders have made use of the low cost of capital to make necessary fiscal adjustments in their economies. In its latest *World Economic Outlook*, the International Monetary Fund (IMF) warns that "beyond the next couple of years, as output gaps close and monetary policy settings continue to normalize, growth in most advanced economies is expected to decline to well below the averages reached before the financial crisis of a decade ago."[11] The IMF also highlights the potential for a slowing of growth in China and other Asian economies. The overarching conclusion is that with "shrinking excess capacity and mounting downsides risks, many countries need to rebuild fiscal buffers and strengthen their resilience to an environment in which financial conditions could tighten suddenly and sharply."[12]

This outlook is absolutely critical to market stability and continued prosperity. It will define rates of economic growth, the balance of economic dynamism worldwide, the level of productivity, the degree of employment, government, corporate

---

10 WTO, Remarks by Director General Roberto Azevêdo, Trade Policy Review Body: Overview of developments in the international trading environment," December 11, 2018.

11 IMF, "Challenges to Steady Growth, *World Economic Outlook* (Washington, DC: IMF, October 2018).

12 *Ibid.*

and private debt overhangs, and the economic prospects for future generations. Every single one of these elements will be highly relevant to corporations. They will surely shape the future of procurement.

Impact of Exponential Technologies

There are few words in the business vocabulary these days that strike fear as much as "digital." As fuzzy as it is, "digital" has come to represent the massive wave of digitalization now transforming all organizations—public and private, big and small, complex and straight-forward, global and local. It symbolizes the prospect of more ambitious goals, higher efficiencies, faster operating speeds, and higher impact. At the same time, the term carries with it serious concerns about dislocations, security issues, higher complexities, the pressure of greater costs, and the constant need to reframe thinking and planning about the theory of organization.

Above all, the fashionable mantra of "digital" reaffirms the prevailing view that we have also reached an "end of era" point when it comes to technological innovation and diffusion.

In our view, there are seven areas of technology that are transforming the fundamental nature of business as we now know it, including the way we work, source, design, produce, market, supply, invest and consume. Together, in a relatively short period of time, these "exponential" technologies could also change the way we live, the quality and longevity of our lives, the kind of data, information, and knowledge we use, the ways in which we communicate and interact with one another, what we eat and drink, the ways that we entertain ourselves, and the ways in which we govern ourselves, our companies, our organizations, and our governments. In a relatively short period of time, the new technologies might even redefine what it means to be human. Think of the 2018 claims from China regarding the birth of twin girls who were "genetically edited."[13]

We can call these the "5 + 2" technology transformations, on grounds that there are five production-related technologies (artificial intelligence (AI), Internet of Things (IOT), 3D printing/additive manufacturing, augmented reality, and advanced robotics) linked to two other crucial tech areas, which are nanotechnology and biotechnology. The upshot is that individually and collectively, these technologies could abruptly alter the entire value chain for organizations the world over. Certainly, they need to be at the center of thinking for leaders in extended supply chains and procurement.

Recently, Kearney worked closely with the World Economic Forum on its "Shaping the Future of Production" initiative — which analyzes how much production-relevant technologies will transform the very nature of production

---

13 In November 2018, immediately prior to the Second International Summit on Human Genome Editing, Chinese scientist He Jiankui (attached to the Southern University of Science and Technology) announced that he had successfully "edited" the genomes of two babies when they were embryos by using the groundbreaking CRISPR-Cas9 technique. See, for example, "Chinese Scientist Claims to Use Crispr to Make First Genetically Edited Babies," *The New York Times*, November 26, 2018.

through 2030.[14] The point of departure for the analysis is that in the fourth industrial revolution,[15] five "exponential" technologies can and likely will permanently alter the production landscape:

- *Artificial intelligence (AI)*: At the core of the ongoing remarkable advances in AI is the continued breathtaking progress in computational speeds and capacities. The current (and fast-changing) assessment of the fastest supercomputers places the Oak Ridge Summit at the top of the list—at 122 petaflops, or 122 quadrillion calculations per second. As staggering as this level is, the introduction of quantum computing systems may soon provide significantly faster speeds. This implies an even faster evolution from "narrow" AI, in which machines outperform humans in narrow functions, to "general" AI, in which machines are able to successfully integrate multiple areas of function. All the while, they will be *en route* to "super" AI—machine-learning at the level where machines can teach themselves and outperform humans at virtually every level.
- *Internet of Things (IoT)*: Propelled by the advances in AI, the IoT is also growing rapidly. Recently released projections suggest that worldwide spending on IoT may reach 1.2 trillion dollars by 2022. The installed base of IoT devices is expected to rise from 27 billion in 2017 to 73 billion in 2025.[16] These and other forecasts emphasize in no uncertain terms the transformative nature of the growing universe of connected devices. Soon more things around us will be connected than are not. For business, the advances in IoT will serve as the foundation for sweeping digital transformations in which they will optimize existing models of operation as well as innovate for the future.
- *Additive manufacturing/3D printing*: According to a recent report, the market for industrial applications for 3D printing could reach 6 billion dollars by 2022 and 7 billion dollars by 2024 with a CAGR of 27 between 2015 and 2024.[17] What has brought the technology to the take-off point is the proliferation in materials that can be printed. The menu of materials that can be printed, which formerly was restricted mainly to plastics and resins, now includes metals and even bio-material.

---

14 See World Economic Forum, *Future of Production* (▶ https://www.weforum.org/communities/the-future-of-production). See also World Economic Forum, "Shaping the Future of Production," ▶ https://www.weforum.org/system-initiatives/shaping-the-future-of-production. The purpose of the "system" initiative is to provide a global, diverse and dynamic platform for leaders to understand the transformation of production systems, develop new and unique value for their organizations and drive the application of technologies to build more innovative, sustainable and inclusive production systems that benefit all.

15 See Klaus Schwab and Nicholas Davis, *Shaping the Fourth Industrial Revolution* (Geneva: World Economic Forum, January 15, 2018).

16 Louis Columbus, "2018 Roundup Of Internet Of Things Forecasts And Market Estimates," *Forbes* ▶ https://www.forbes.com/sites/louiscolumbus/2018/12/13/2018-roundup-of-internet-of-things-forecasts-and-market-estimates/#4a9abd307d83

17 "Additive Manufacturing Market is Expected to Exceed U.S.$ 6 billion by 2022," *MarketWatch*, December 16, 2018 ▶ https://www.marketwatch.com/press-release/additive-manufacturing-market-is-expected-to-exceed-us-6-billion-by-2022-2018-08-06

- *Augmented reality (AR)*: The integration of business training and operational functions associated with artificial reality and virtual reality (VR) is growing rapidly. Here, too, the numbers begin to tell the story. Worldwide spending on AR and VR is expected to be 17.8 billion dollars in 2018, up from 9.1 billion dollars in 2017.[18]
- *Advanced robotics*: The global balance of power in the use of industrial robots has shifted rapidly from western countries to Asia and is forever changing the business model underpinning global value chains. A recent report has documented this shift, revealing that select economies (South Korea, Singapore and Germany, followed by Japan, Sweden and Denmark) have the highest levels of industrial robots in the world.[19] The report also says that on a "wage-adjusted basis, Southeast Asian nations lead the world in robot adoption, occupying six of the top seven positions in the ranking." The report said South Korea leads the world with 2.4 times more robots adopted than expected, followed in order by Singapore, Thailand, China, and Taiwan."[20]

Of course, tomes can and will be written regarding these and other technology trends transforming the business landscape. The point of outlining them here is to emphasize how important they will be in defining the contours of the global economy of the future—and to decisions involving procurement.

Two additional points regarding this technology transformation need to be emphasized. The first is that levels of national "readiness" regarding these exponential technologies vary greatly. The economies that are able to pre-position themselves to thrive in this altered tech environment—and all the adjacent changes it engenders—will be in a position to prosper. Those left behind will likely face extremely difficult circumstances.

To measure the respective levels of national readiness, Kearney undertook a country-by-country assessment of some 100 economies around the world as part of its collaboration with the World Economic Forum. The results (see ◖ Fig. 1.1) indicated that within the four quadrants of the future, ranging from least-prepared to most-prepared, only 25 countries in Europe, North America, and East Asia were positioned to benefit from the changing nature of production.

The second point is that from the standpoint of global value chains, this shifting balance may translate into a "re-shuffling of the global production cards" that have been so fundamental to procurement and management of extended supply chains for the past quarter century and beyond. Further, recent changes put at risk

---

18 "Worldwide Spending on Augmented and Virtual Reality Forecast to Reach $17.8 Billion in 2018, According to IDC," *BusinessWire*, November 29, 2017 ► https://www.businesswire.com/news/home/20171129005097/en/Worldwide Spending-Augmented-Virtual-Reality-Forecast-Reach

19 Robert D. Atkinson, "Which Nations Really Lead in Industrial Robot Adoption?" ITIF ► https://itif.org/publications/2018/11/19/which-nations-really-lead-industrial-robot-adoption

20 See Sintia Radu, "Too Few Robots in the West Compared to Asia: When it comes to automation, advanced economies are not the ones performing best," *U.S. News & World Report*, December 5 ► https://www.usnews.com/news/best-countries/articles/2018-12-05/too-few-robots-in-the-west-compared-to-asia-research-says

1

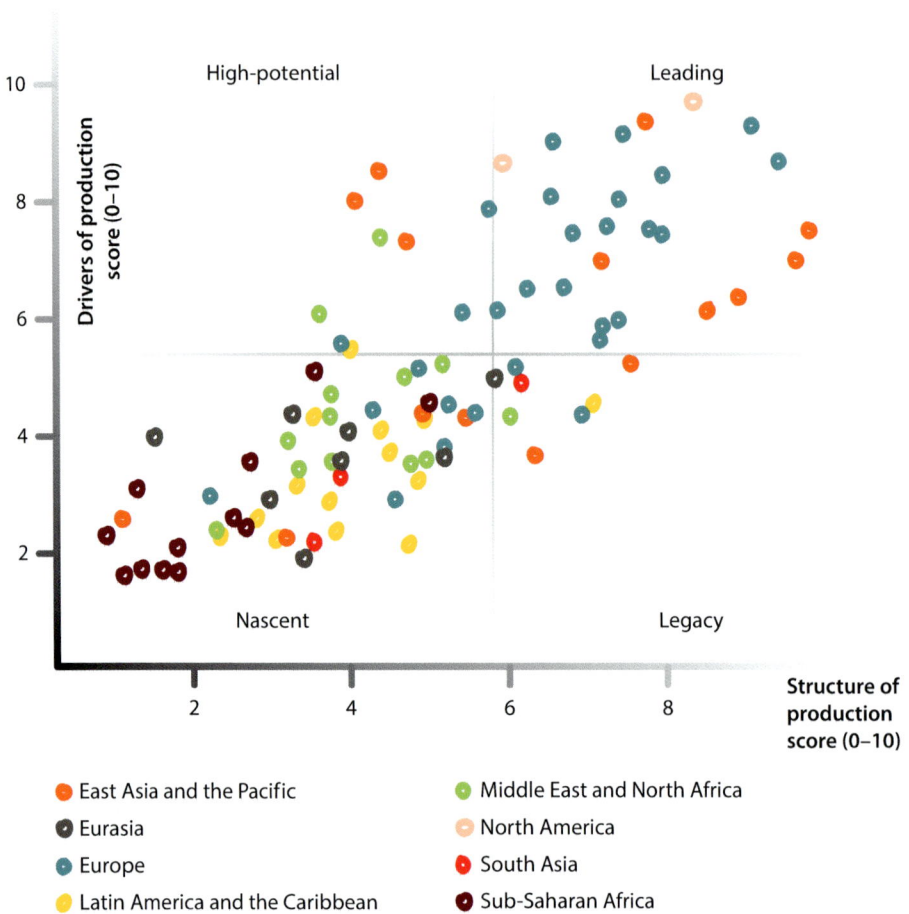

◘ Fig. 1.1 Readiness of countries to benefit from changes in production. **Note**: Average performance of the top 75 countries is at the intersection of the four quadrants

the competitiveness paradigm of low-cost manufacturing exports as a means for growth and development. Of particular relevance to business will be the capacity of national law and regulatory systems to keep up with the hyper-change that goes with these technologies. Those national systems that can put into place conducive environments for the next generation of production will likely see significant returns on investment.

Eroding Institutions and the Decay of Public Trust

The final outgoing era can be linked to the ongoing deterioration—or even rapid decay—of institutions and practices that have defined economics and commerce for centuries. The list of "extinct" structures—governments, companies, academic institutions, and non-governmental organizations that have failed to keep up with changes in the theory of their business—is growing by the day. Leader after leader has failed to heed the warning made by consulting guru Peter Drucker in his now-famous article that appeared in the *Harvard Business Review* nearly a quarter century ago:

» The root cause of nearly every one of these crises is not that things are being done poorly. It is not even that the wrong things are being done. Indeed, in most cases, the right things are being done—but fruitlessly. What accounts for this apparent paradox? The assumptions on which the organization has been built and is being run no longer fit reality. These are the assumptions that shape any organization's behavior, dictate its decisions about what to do and what not to do, and define what the organization considers meaningful results.[21]

Moreover, many more existing organizations are becoming progressively dysfunctional and obsolete. In the government sphere, certainly, the pressures on democracies have been growing steadily. Freedom House, for example, chose to assign the name "Democracy in Crisis" to its latest *Freedom in the World* assessment.[22] And for good reason. It points to the "12th consecutive year of decline in global freedom" and notes that since 2006, democracies have been in decline.[23]

Furthermore, the rise of nationalism and populism has been evident in countries across the world. In many cases, traditional political institutions and practices have been overshadowed by what embattled groups believe is the incapacity of established structures to adopt to new opportunities and challenges. In the corporate sphere, companies falling short of seeing fundamental shifts in the theory of their business have paid a massive price. From Kodak's decision to forgo development of digital photos to preserve its film business, to the decision at Blockbuster not to focus on the meteoric rise of Netflix, to the inability at Nokia to embrace the smartphone, the examples of epic declines reflect a significant disruption in business models that leaders could not anticipate or act on.

Moving and unifying stakeholders who may have unaligned or even conflicting points of view has always been a difficult proposition. But under the current circumstances, in which social media and other technology-enabled social mobilization has made the gaps between many groups all the more profound, fewer and fewer leaders have the "right stuff" to reverse the centrifugal forces at play. Moisés Naim, in his book provocatively entitled *The End of Power: From Boardrooms to Battlefields and Churches to States, Why Being in Charge Isn't What It Used to Be*, has it precisely right when he argues that in the twenty-first century, "power is easier to get, harder to use—and easier to lose."[24] By extension, for these reasons, the challenge of leadership has become all the more daunting.

---

21 Peter F. Drucker, "The Theory of the Business," *Harvard Business Review*, Sept-Oct 1994.
22 Freedom House, *Freedom in the World 2018*.
23 Michael J. Abramowitz, "Democracy in Crisis," *Freedom in the World 2018*, p. 1.
24 Moises Naim, *The End of Power: From Boardrooms to Battlefields and Churches to States, Why Being in Charge Isn't What It Used to Be* (New York, Basic Books, 2013), p. 2.

1

One of the main underlying reasons for the mounting public ennui regarding globalization is the growing level of disparity or even inequality within societies. In a number of societies, high levels of resentment are undercutting the legitimacy of institutions and resulting in populist positions and policies. Often times, the growth of this kind of corrosive populist opinion can manifest itself in a more sweeping renunciation of institutions—from governments to business to media.

The Edelman Trust Barometer is a valuable annual indicator of changes in the way the populations in 28 countries regard the institutions around them. In the results for 2018, there is compelling evidence for what Edelman refers to as the "fourth wave of the trust tsunami"—the loss of trust in information and information sources.[25] The earlier waves leading to loss of trust were: (1) job insecurity resulting from globalization and automation brought about by technology; (2) the far-reaching negative effects of the Great Recession; and (3) the impact of migration.[26]

The latest results indicate that a significant majority of general populations in the countries surveyed—that is, all respondents without university/college education and below the top 25 percent in income—distrust their institutions. In fact, 20 of the 28 countries surveyed were considered to distrust institutions.

As ◘ Fig. 1.2 shows, the overall level of "general population" trust of institutions is low. Government and the media have the lowest scores in 2018, at 43 percent. Business and non-governmental organizations (NGOs) scored roughly ten points higher. The message here is crystal clear, however. The strong majority of countries surveyed have populations that distrust their institutions. Leaders need to be acutely aware that they are navigating in this environment.

The Repercussions for Globalization: Imagining the Future

At the center of the uncertainties is the phenomenon that has contributed so greatly to the trajectory of the global economy: globalization. Globalization has transformed the business environment for the past quarter century, and—at least until the onset of the Great Recession in 2007—business and political leaders took for granted the continued growth in cross-border movement of economic factors: trade in goods and services, direct and portfolio capital, people and labor, and intellectual property.

---

25 See Richard Edelman, 2018 Edelman Trust Barometer, Executive Summary, January 2018
   ▶ https://www.edelman.com/sites/g/files/aatuss191/files/2018-10/2018_Edelman_Trust_
   Barometer_Global_Report_FEB.pdf
26 *Ibid.*, p. 2.

Trust in Institutions

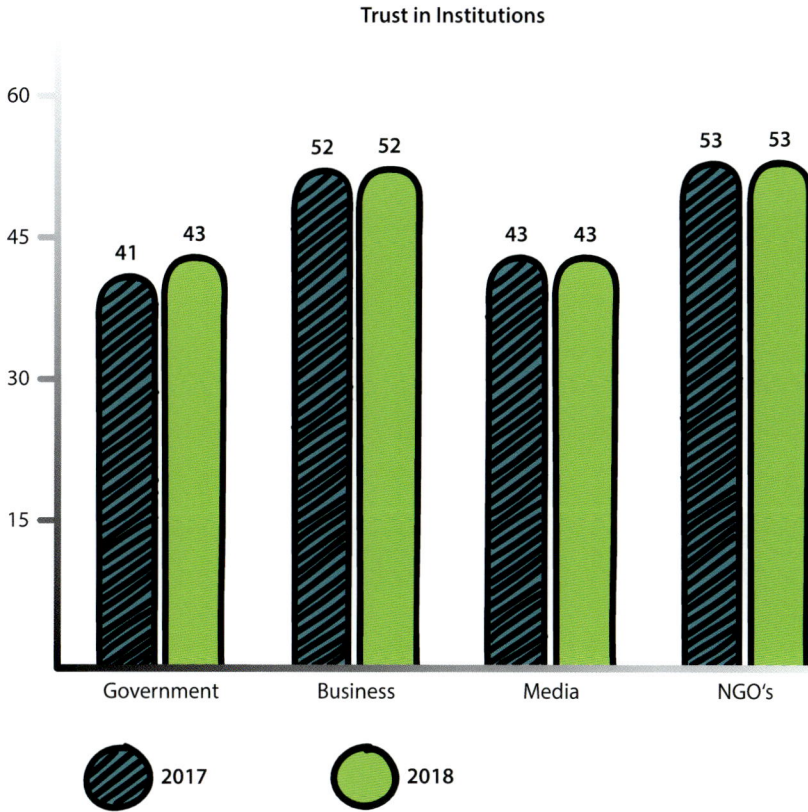

Fig. 1.2 Trust in institutions: Edelman Trust Barometer. (From the 2018 Edelman Trust Barometer (▶ https://www.edelman.com/trust-barometer)). Percent trust in each type of institution. Change from 2017 to 2018. A global study by Edelman. N = 32,200

The reality, however, is that a decade after the Great Recession, the 2018 flows in most categories are only now reaching their pre-recession levels. Aside from the savage effects of the sharp economic downturn, there were also the more enduring social effects that would weigh on the process. In 2008, Henry Kissinger described globalization in this way: "For the first time in history, a genuinely global economic system has come into being with prospects of heretofore unimagined well-being. At the same time—paradoxically—the process of globalization tempts a nationalism that threatens its fulfillment."[27]

As we look to the future of procurement, then, it is necessary to consider— and plan for—alternative and plausible futures that might materialize. Kearney's

---

27 Henry A. Kissinger, "Globalization and its Discontents," *The New York Times*, May 28, 2008.

1

Global Business Policy Council has released precisely such a study outlining how four compelling and contrasting futures might materialize.[28] We call them "Globalization 3.0," "Polarization," "Islandization" and "Commonization."

- If what we call *"Globalization 3.0"* were to be the new future, the world would return to the high levels of economic growth and trade of the early 2000s (pre-Great Recession). Commodity prices would be low, prosperity high, and improvements in information and communications technologies would continue to be commonplace.
- The second paradigm, *"Polarization,"* would set up the world in political and economic rivalries and divide the global economy into competing blocs of countries.
- *"Islandization"* is the third potential future. If this were to occur, nationalism will have gained ground in key economies around the world, leading to dramatic protectionist measures and drastically reduced global economic flows.
- The fourth possible future, *"Commonization,"* represents a greater break from the past than ever before, with the rise of a new global commons through the continued rise of additive manufacturing and the sharing economy. This would be a future in which millennials, many of whom base their decision-making on altruistic considerations, would prevail in terms of policy and consumer-preference.

No matter which of these potential outcomes materializes, the world is arguably more segmented and defensive than in the past. It becomes a place in which populations are uncomfortable with the status quo and afraid of their futures—with particular concern about the role of technology in the workplace (including automation), the impact of continued migration, and the collapse of institutions. In ◼ Fig. 1.3, we speculate on the impact of these contrasting environments on a number of important short-term variables. The current circumstances seem to suggest that we are moving toward a world that is progressively polarized, even islandized. It remains to be seen how leaders can adapt to the profound forces of change that we have described briefly, but the pendulum appears to be swinging to the revival of populist nationalism. In the final analysis, what the economists Carmen Reinhart and Kenneth Rogoff observed about the history of financial crises in their book applies to each of these potential narratives: Although leaders invariably claim that "this time is different," the financial consequences strike with surprisingly consistent frequency, duration and ferocity.[29]

---

28 Paul A. Laudicina and Erik R. Peterson, *From Globalization to Islandization* (Kearney Global Business Policy Council, January 2016). See also Paul A. Laudicina, Erik R. Peterson, Peter Munro, and Robert Holt, World Out of Balance: Challenges and Opportunities for Australia (Kearney Global Business Policy Council (Washington, DC, 2017).

29 Carmen M. Reinhart & Kenneth S. Rogoff, *This Time Is Different: Eight Centuries of Financial Folly* (Princeton, NJ: Princeton University Press, 2009).

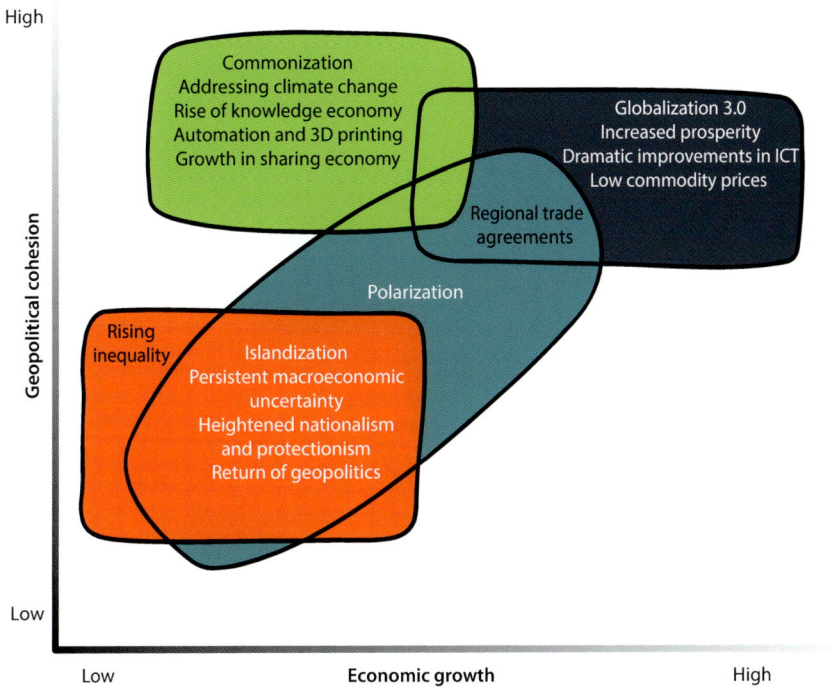

◘ Fig. 1.3 From Globalization to Islandization. **Note**: ICT is information and communication technologies

The Challenge of the Disruptive Environment to Disruptive Procurement

What do these forces of change mean for multinational companies and the procurement function, as seen in ◘ Fig. 1.4?

In his "What if?" column, Thomas Friedman concludes with what he characterizes as the worst "what if" of all: "What if we're having a presidential election but no one is even asking these questions, let alone "what if" all of these tectonic plates move at once? How will we generate growth, jobs, security and resilience?"[30]

In procurement, leaders need to be asking their own questions. Are these sweeping changes plausible? If yes, when might they happen? How will circumstances change in the meantime—before the tectonic forces actually converge to reshape

---

30　*Ibid.*

1

	Globalization 3.0	Polarization	Islandization	Commonization
Economic growth	High	Moderate	Low	Low
Unemployment	Low	Moderate	Moderate	Low
Inequality	Moderate	Moderate	High	Low
Trade flows	High	Moderate	Low	Moderate
Capital flows	High	Moderate	Low	Low
International migration	High	Moderate	Low	Low
Regulatory convergence	High	Moderate	Low	Low

Fig. 1.4   Global growth and interconnectedness per alternative future

markets and realities? What are the consequences of a mistake in judgment? And how will all these elements affect competitors?

Disruptive Procurement leaders, in order to address the disruptive setting within which they will be operating, will need to begin by addressing five important priorities:

- *Put surveillance into place*: The first-order priority must be to monitor ongoing change, either to validate current assumptions or to revisit strategies and actions that may not be aligned with shifting circumstances. To do this, it means putting together a robust conceptual framework with clear-cut roles and responsibilities on what needs to be observed, what benchmarks might suggest the onset of a transition, and how signals (faint or otherwise) can and should be communicated within the organization. In addition, establishing a network of subject-matter experts and independent organizations relating to the content of the surveillance can often provide welcome returns.
- *Double down on strategic foresight*: Many of the quantitative tools and empirical approaches long associated with procurement make it challenging to integrate strategic foresight, which more times than not is qualitatively based, but it

is nevertheless extremely important. Strategic foresight may include visioning, trends analysis, scenario planning or crowdsourcing, and it challenges procurement planners to consider contingencies that might not arise in their normal day-to-day operations. Even with advanced quantitative tools and analytics, the gaps in prediction capabilities have been abundantly clear in recent years—from the Great Recession, to Brexit, to the election of Donald Trump.[31] As the oft-quoted saying goes, "it is better to be imprecisely right rather than precisely wrong." Planning for multiple futures makes sense in the light of all the complexities we have highlighted here.

- *Strengthen organizational agility*: Even if robust surveillance and strategic foresight capabilities are developed, if the organization is unable (or unwilling) to respond quickly and effectively, it defeats the point. Authentically "disruptive" procurement means constantly innovating on established practices in order to take advantage of accelerating change. As this constellation of changes materializes, chances are that the stakes will rise—and the difference between winners and losers will become increasingly profound. The priority, therefore, must be to connect foresight with action in such a way that the organization can respond effectively. Those falling short, especially in the face of the totality of change ahead, are likely to become roadkill.
- *Redefine risk management*: Procurement leaders must now consider the full spectrum of forces at work—and the reverberations of all the eras that are now ending—by expanding their aperture on both the risk-mitigation and opportunity-leveraging sides of their operations. On the risk-mitigation side, that means addressing current-time operational risk as well as pushing the envelope as far out as possible on future risks and strategies to cope. It is the same on the opportunities side: "Eat-what-you-kill" attitudes may suffice in the short term, but longer-range strategies necessarily must depend on more proactive planning and execution.
- *Reinvent your culture*: Failure to adjust to changing circumstances could be life-threatening. Effective leaders have managed to implement visions across their organizations that ultimately become a part of the corporate culture. This is especially applicable to Disruptive Procurement—a core feature of which is a fundamental reset of the mindset that leaders have had in the past. The challenge to leaders is to implant an authentically strategic DNA in their operations that will position their teams to succeed in the future.

In the end, procurement planners can either carefully consider the menu, or they can be on it. Procurement leaders understand that more widely integrated, more proactive, more inclusive actions are essential for them to get ahead in this time of disruptive change in the external environment.

---

31 See, for example, Rudolph Lohmeyer, Erik R. Peterson, and Paul A. Laudicina, *No One Saw it Coming: Strategic foresight is a powerful tool for managing uncertainty in an age of disruption*, Kearney Global Business Policy Council ► https://www.kearney.com/web/global-business-policy-council/article?/a/no-one-saw-it-coming

The Future of Procurement

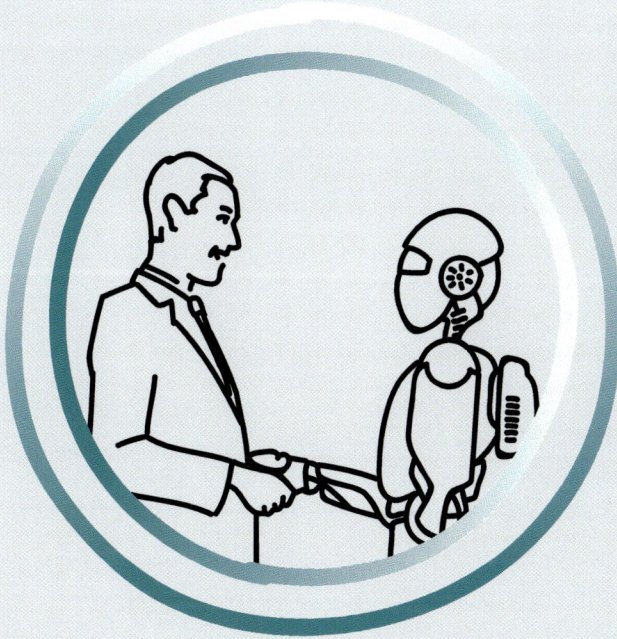

Contents

© Springer Nature Switzerland AG 2020
M. F. Strohmer et al., *Disruptive Procurement*, https://doi.org/10.1007/978-3-030-38950-5_2

A New Operating Model for Procurement

Procurement has languished toward obsolescence and will die without a transformation. That means that today's Chief Procurement Officers (CPOs) have just one job: adopt a future-focused model to meet users' needs.

Over the past few years, we have received a litany of calls from clients saying they have spent millions of dollars on their procurement technology suites, and across the board, the solutions have failed to live up to what was promised. Bad user experiences, incomplete functionality, and a lack of advanced features were just a few of the many issues they discussed. Many companies have asked us what to do.

Inexplicably, this steady stream of frustrations came at a time when "digital procurement" was a hot topic. Spurred by the digital revolution of big data, robotic process automation, artificial intelligence (AI), and blockchain, a flood of hype promised to bring procurement into the twenty-first century.

Exploring this dichotomy set us on a journey to better understand how companies are embracing—or not embracing—their legacy systems, what real innovations are emerging in the market, and how procurement organizations should organize to prepare for the future. We co-created a vision with our clients and external networks. Taken together, the insights have become the foundation of our Future of Procurement series of articles. It started as a set of thought-provoking, provocative articles to spur conversations and break complacency with the status quo. The response has been overwhelmingly positive as our articles tapped into a deep well of frustration and resentment. For example, we posited that "current procurement technology is an abject failure, totally not fit for purpose. Everyone hates it." That turned out to be an unassailable truth for many.

In our examination of market trends, we discovered there has been nearly 500 million dollars of venture capital invested in procurement technology startups over the past five years—a staggering sum considering that less than a decade ago, everyone seemed to think the market was mature. But in exploring what these startups are focused on, we made a stunning discovery. Nearly three-quarters of them are solving problems from the early 2000s: spend visibility, supplier rationalization, and basic sourcing were the common themes. This got us wondering: where did all the fancy digital technology go? Turns out that part of the equation remains unaccounted for and thus an opportunity.

Identifying the issues was easy; the hard part was identifying the implications. How will digital technology impact direct versus indirect procurement activities? What type of talent will be needed, and why should CEOs care? Will procurement as a function continue to exist? These are just a few of the questions we address here. Simultaneously, there are market forces at play as legacy players, such as Emptoris, exit the space and SAP retires older versions of Ariba. Perhaps the biggest question is when will the corporate buying experience be like shopping on Amazon? In that vein, one CEO has asked, "Why can we not just have an app that does procurement for us?" It's a fair question.

A good place to begin this discussion about unrealized "digital disruption" and the future of procurement is by getting back to the basics and understanding fundamental problems.

2

In our view, one very basic problem is that procurement organizations around the world are struggling to keep their internal customers satisfied. In fact, many procurement organizations are more of a barrier than a benefit. Today's consumers are deeply familiar with online platforms such as Amazon, where buying is simple and fast, and they have come to expect a seamless buying process with full transparency on product details, prices, alternatives, and delivery information. And yet, these same consumers often face complex, opaque purchasing processes when they are at work. An array of business stakeholders, including Chief Financial Officers (CFOs), are beginning to clamor for change as they question the value of procurement.

As technology such as AI, blockchain, and advanced analytics move into the mainstream, procurement's low-value repeatable work such as simply processing orders is rapidly being automated or displaced. However, many of these advancements are still trying to solve the same spend-transparency challenges that were top-of-mind two decades ago.

Even today, procurement is only at its best when it handles regular purchases with simple specifications. It stumbles with irregular purchases and complex specifications for several reasons:

— Specification is an art. Usually, procurement is barely involved in specifying for direct categories. Specialist functional experts—often engineers or operations managers—typically indicate what they want. For indirect categories such as marketing, professional, or legal services and technology, the story is the same.
— Irregular purchases are still challenging. Current systems and processes do not cope well with one-offs from a transactional perspective.
— The ability of data analytics to identify patterns and deduce trends that can be acted upon is still low. For example, procurement struggles to drive value from tail spend yet slows down users by forcing them to follow complex and broken administrative processes.

Even when companies have sourced effectively and agreed on contractual terms, they often fail to adhere to those terms or buy on contract, which leads to "maverick" spending.

Procurement functions then claim "savings" that are often unrealistic and which do not end up on the bottom line. At the same time, the impact of inflation is often ignored. This reduces credibility with senior executives. One CEO we know tells the story of a procurement function that claimed savings that were greater each year than the entire profit of the organization. This behavior is unhelpful and adds to the "noise."

Amid the escalating expectations of consumers and the companies they work for, procurement is at risk of collapsing under the weight of its own complexity. Forward-thinking procurement must turn its attention to its primary purpose: translating supply–market value into product value for the end customer. The main tenets of this kind of Disruptive Procurement have largely been forgotten in the day-to-day busy work of common desktop activities such as negotiating savings, managing risk, ensuring legal compliance, processing transactions, and managing categories. Although there is nothing wrong with these activities, they have come to define the discipline instead of being tools in a larger toolbox.

Enter Tangible Disruptive Procurement

The future of procurement will require an innovative operating model and advanced skills. Disruptive Procurement relies on three pillars.
- *Strategic sourcing* determines what to buy and from where, through effective use of supply and demand power.
- *Supplier management* ensures that what is contracted for is what is actually delivered and then collaborates with the supplier to bring in more supply-market expertise to drive the right supplier behaviors.
- Finally, *advanced technology and processes* provide a frictionless, compliance-based buying experience.

All too often, these pillars are abandoned because the organization lacks the basic insights and understanding to harness supply-market power, fails to adequately track supplier performance, and lacks the talent to design an advanced system. As a result, too much attention is paid to costs, arguing over contract terms, and insisting on control over every aspect of the buying process. Administration, rigid processes, and complexity have often reigned supreme at the expense of function, utility and the ultimate needs of the business.

To be fair, procurement is not alone in this. Other supporting business functions have been mired in similar under-developed environments. Finance spends much of its energy on bookkeeping rather than driving effective capital utilization. Human resources spends a great deal of time on processes and administration rather than motivating and enabling the workforce. IT focuses on what users can do or not do, instead of harnessing the power of technology to help the business compete. However, this situation will change dramatically as companies begin to use transformative digital technology.

Procurement Technology Is Coming of Age

In many ways, today's procurement organizations resemble white-collar versions of manufacturing in the 1970s. Manual processes still dominate, even as automation transforms other business functions. Legions of staffers handle low-value sourcing and demand-management activities, where they have leverage over suppliers and the ability to influence users. Routine, labor-intensive transactional activities such as pricing negotiations, contract awards, and supplier performance monitoring consume time and attention. Procurement workers spend hours piecing together fragmented information flows from myriad transactions—a task technology could perform in seconds. Meanwhile, internal stakeholders grow frustrated by what they perceive as slow service, yearning for self-service options and direct access to more comprehensive information about the purchasing process.

All this is about to change. Procurement is ripe for reinvention with digital technologies on pace to automate and create transparency for most routine processes within three to five years. A convergence of AI, advanced analytics, and other new technologies will automate manual processes and empower business

2

users with the tools and information to get what they need—without help from procurement. However, forward-thinking procurement organizations are looking beyond automation, transparency, and simply cutting costs. Digitalization has the power to unleash a wealth of new value sources and give procurement a much larger strategic role.

Automation fuels efficiency and creates opportunities for procurement to add value in areas that can't be automated. Like production managers in a modern digital factory, procurement leaders can orchestrate end-to-end processes with a strategic perspective and an eye on long-term value. As technology takes over routine transactional work, they can focus on higher-value activities such as forming vendor partnerships and re-engineering products.

The future of procurement looks familiar in some ways and strikingly different in others. The function will always meet basic needs such as selecting suppliers, but digitally enabled procurement teams will play a larger role in advancing corporate strategies by improving products and services and turning supplier capabilities into a competitive advantage.

It may be tempting to dismiss advances such as AI as just another wave of over-hyped technologies. After all, the tools that software vendors such as SAP and IBM have rolled out have barely touched procurement. Today, few processes are fully automated, and end-to-end information transparency is limited. Although large global manufacturers have automated replenishment and other direct spending categories, manual processes persist for indirect expenditures, and many companies have yet to automate all direct categories.

Blame traditional software vendors' sluggish innovation or procurement stakeholders' resistance to technology—or both—but lagging technology adoption is holding the function back. Procurement organizations often can't fully use their sourcing software, and many chief procurement officers are left hoping that major vendors will someday offer a valuable user-friendly option.

The technological tipping point is here. AI, blockchain, and the Internet of Things (IoT) are transforming how we interact with technology, and they're converging to form autonomous procurement tools that will run the entire procure-to-pay process, including generating contracts. Data input and classification will become much more accurate when intelligent systems start executing transactions independently. In fact, some companies already use AI to classify spend. Even more impressive is the potential of AI and blockchain to track contract compliance in real time, a feat nearly impossible for today's archaic systems.

The implications are profound. For a glimpse of the future, consider technology's impact on corporate IT departments over the past two decades. Automation didn't disrupt IT overnight but encroached slowly and subtly. Back in 2000, data centers were staffed by well-paid systems administrators with advanced technical skills who kept IT networks running smoothly. It was hands-on work overseeing fleets of on-site servers that were manually racked and locally managed. Most companies had one systems administrator for every 10 servers. A decade later, the ratio had dropped to one administrator for every 100 servers as virtualization and cloud computing transformed IT infrastructure. Humans were still involved, but automated systems made basic tasks such as deploying new servers and responding to problems as simple as point and click. Today's IT systems are largely self-managing, self-diagnosing, and self-repairing. AI tracks usage, decides when to add capacity, deploys new servers, spots trouble, and repairs machines—with no human intervention. Today's ratio of systems administrators to servers? One to 35,000. The few remaining administrators keep tabs on automated systems that do the work they used to do. In less than two decades, technological progress has all but eliminated a lucrative, high-skill career.

Procurement is moving down the same path. Automation and information transparency continue to expand, especially in categories where companies have the economic leverage to force vendors to adopt new technologies. The future looks bleak for procurement workers who handle the low-value work of basic negotiations, writing statements of work, and churning out reports. Software will take over these tasks and empower users with the information they need to make their own decisions. As employment levels shrink, talent requirements will shift, favoring people who know how to solve problems and work across functional boundaries. Procurement's focus will turn to categories that are more intrinsic to the product offer where suppliers have more power and more to offer, increasing demand for skills such as rethinking specifications and managing negotiations and alliances.

Reinventing Procurement

So far, procurement technology has been a disappointment. Business and procurement users alike loathe it, and technology vendors treat procurement as a second-class citizen. In fact, after years of technology deployment, most organizations still struggle to get a comprehensive view of their spending. The systems are rigid and complicated, and they only meet a fraction of procurement's requirements.

Across the board, these systems curtail progress and hinder excellence instead of enabling it. For anything other than simple pre-specified and pre-sourced catalog-based purchases, for example, systems do not help the user specify what is required or choose the right supplier. They also don't help in finding out what the price should be. And there is usually no systematic, embedded classification of what was actually purchased so trends can be identified and managed in a timely manner. What emerges is an inability to know where money is being spent and with whom, much less an ability to strategically direct that spending. This puts procurement into a backward-looking mode at a time when looking ahead is crucial.

So how did we get here? Today's procurement technology landscape is based on a linear concept of sourcing and procure-to-pay activities with a bit of analytics and governance thrown in. Traditional suites are nice, neat packages, but they reflect little about the reality of day-to-day procurement, and they have forgotten the main goal of procurement: transforming goods and services into corporate value. After nearly two decades of failure, tech vendors are finally waking up to this.

The Beginnings of a Procurement Revolution

Despite the bleakness of procurement suite solutions, several effective technology startups have emerged over the past few years. For example, Scout burst onto the scene in 2014 with a fresh take on sourcing tools built on modern architectures and

2

updated sourcing concepts. The sourcing functionality is comparable to previous systems, but it is much more intuitive, faster and easier to use. Advanced analytics companies such as Tamr are applying machine learning to challenges such as spend management and complexity reduction. Consequently, the once-onerous analysis of tail spend is vastly sped up and simplified, potentially unlocking opportunities worth tens of millions of dollars.

A cynic might look at these new startups and conclude that they will be gobbled up by the big suite companies. However, there is a fundamental reason why this may not happen. The software development industry has gone through its own transformation during the past decade, creating a new foundational architecture in the process. Based on cloud technology, it is designed around microservices supporting application programming interfaces. These microservices allow apps to seamlessly connect to one another, enabling the easy and seamless exchange of information across applications. These advancements give users the best possible functionality and the ability to quickly—and ideally, cheaply—modify as needed. The traditional functions in the rigid linear process are now distributed through an extendible ecosystem that allows for very precise, and even overlapping, use of best-of-breed technologies.

For example, a procurement organization could use Sievo for spend analytics while also using Tamr for tail-spend management. Traditional systems such as procure-to-pay (P2P) will still be required and will not go away, but instead of being closed systems, they will open up into a broader more flexible ecosystem. Underpinning this new architecture is an AI hub that can serve as the integration point and drive the push toward automation. This will require suite providers to change their long-term strategies, which will be counter to their short-term revenue models. However, there will be plenty of opportunities for them to not only survive but excel. Their individual components will still be relevant, but they will be required to compete in the open market and will lose their ability to lock customers into a proprietary offering.

It is not possible to predict precisely which products and which vendors will succeed in the future. However, we believe that the technology landscape of the future may look like ◘ Fig. 2.1, with an ecosystem of interconnected tools; not a classic linear suite solution.

An App for Procurement?

As mentioned, a CEO recently asked why there isn't an app for procurement? What he really meant was, "Why do I pay for a procurement function when my partner, kids, and nearly every other person who shops online have a frictionless customer experience with a simple click of a button?" While they are shopping, they automatically receive recommendations for other—possibly better—options with instant visibility to compare prices, warranties, shipping options, and customer reviews so they can make an informed choice. Today's consumers can buy almost anything at any time with a nearly unlimited number of choices, which of course encourages people to shop and buy more. The entire buying process is quick and easy.

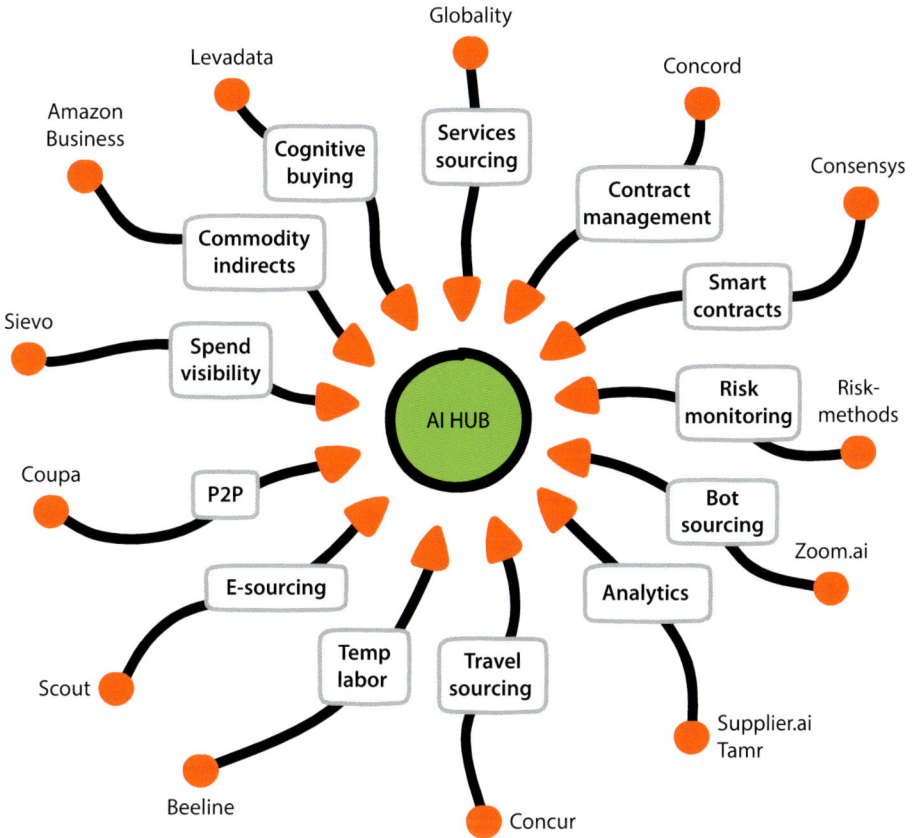

☐ **Fig. 2.1** Possible procurement technology ecosystem: a mosaic connected to an artificial intelligence hub

Now compare that with corporate buying. The experiences could not be any more different. Most corporate purchasing is slow, opaque, and downright onerous—fueled by a broader objective to control spending. Procurement departments work tirelessly to create and maintain corporate catalogs of standard items and employ teams of people to source unique goods and services. This creates several structural problems.

First, for catalog items, there are limitations on the product assortment, warranties, shipping options and prices. These factors are usually negotiated in advance and are not adjusted for market dynamics or a supplier's performance. In addition, catalog systems are labor-intensive to set up and maintain, so while a large portion of spending might take place within the system, the company could be missing out on the advantages of their supply and demand power. For non-standard goods and services, the process is more complicated, often requiring procurement personnel to interject themselves into the buying process despite having no expertise about the product or the supply market. As a result, decision-making is much slower—often with no material improvement to the outcome.

2

Consider this example. A consumer who wants to buy an airline ticket can go to her favorite carrier and look for fares, and if she sees something she likes, she can buy it, or she can go to a travel clearinghouse site and look for a deal that meets her needs. In the corporate world, that buying experience looks much different. For most companies, booking a flight requires either calling an approved travel agent or going to a corporate travel portal that has a list of pre-approved suppliers. The problem is the negotiated rates could be higher than what is happening in the market, not to mention that the process is more time-consuming and complex.

Of course, procurement does still have a role to play. But the fundamental question is why the function is right in the middle of the purchasing process if it is not adding value. Procurement often acts as a quasi-budget control function, operating with the implicit mantra that if buying is difficult, then expenditures will be lower. However, this is the wrong approach. Forward-thinking companies control their budgets while also meeting the needs of the business without impeding productivity. If someone needs to buy something, the process should not only be easy but also add value rather than being a shadowy way to regulate spending.

The Digital Consumer Revolution

The consumer market reveals there is a better way. Corporate procurement should be focused on orchestrating a buying experience that mirrors the consumer experience. When this happens, business users will be much happier with the process, and procurement will be empowered to deliver more value by focusing on activities and spending areas that are strategic to the business. This will require forming close relationships with internal stakeholders as well as strategic partnerships with external suppliers that understand what the company needs. The consumerization of the corporate environment is not a new phenomenon. But in most industries, it has been happening surprisingly slowly. After all, nearly everyone who works in a corporate environment has experienced a frictionless and satisfying digital experience in their private lives—not only through online shopping, but also in social media, gaming, online communities, virtual learning, or simply browsing the Web. The proliferation of easy-to-use devices such as smartphones, tablets, and digital media players, just to name a few, offers users of all ages and skill levels a gratifying way to engage in the digital world.

One driving and practical force of the digital consumer revolution has been the notion of the customer journey—the stages a consumer goes through when interacting with a company. This has put a spotlight on the individual user experience. However, corporate systems have been built around complex business processes or obsolete technology.

Leading organizations are adopting the customer journey approach to redesign their procurement functions. An effective method for enabling this new approach is to use design thinking, which seeks to create a product that delights customers with a frictionless experience. This requires bringing customers into the design process at all stages to ensure their needs are being met. In a corporate environment, this can mean meeting internal customer needs by first asking them about those needs, all while capturing productivity gains, cost savings and a competitive advantage. Not surprisingly, tech companies that offer superior customer journeys—think Amazon, Snapchat, Airbnb, and Apple—excel at design thinking.

Creating Innovative Procurement Processes

Perhaps the greatest indicator of a procurement organization's failure—aside from unhappy users—is the inability to accurately report where money is being spent, if what is being paid matches what was contracted, and how suppliers are performing. And although most organizations claim to have negotiated lower prices, the savings often do not clearly affect profit.

To control external spending and manage supplier risk, many procurement organizations have a complicated set of rigid processes embedded into an archaic set of tools that attempt to control where money is spent and ensure maximum use of pre-negotiated contracts.

Despite these processes, money goes here, there, and everywhere with no actual control. In reality, procurement is seldom able to reconcile spending with the original supplier agreements. Forcing people to use these processes gives the illusion of control, but the reality is that few businesses have controls that actually work—a problem that grows exponentially more complicated for industries with regulatory reporting burdens.

The exception is in areas where control is needed for non-procurement purposes, such as rigid specifications and supplier qualification requirements to achieve quality control. In these cases, procurement usually struggles to address such constraints in a way that drives commercial advantage. However, successful corporate models do exist. Visit a San Francisco Bay Area startup, and, aside from free lunches, dogs, and toy-filled conference rooms, you will likely see an IT vending machine filled with a variety of desktop and smartphone peripherals such as Bluetooth keyboards, earbuds, and flash drives—frequently used items that are there for the taking by any employee who needs them. All they have to do is scan their badge and make their selection.

This is the epitome of trust with verification—giving everyone access to the things they need to do their jobs but preventing anyone from abusing the system. In this model of procurement, controls are based on audits, and since everything is digitally tracked, there is little concern for theft or malfeasance. Besides, the benefits far outweigh the risks. Employees can get the items they need when they need them without having to involve anyone from either procurement or IT, and procurement can tailor the items that are in each vending machine based on the equipment that is used in each office.

Rather than relying on front-end controls that slow down the process, innovative organizations use after-the-event controls that create transparency and data-enabled feedback loops for prioritization. Traditional procurement functions with corporate catalogs, purchasing requisitions, and complex processes are designed on the assumption that procurement's job is to prevent employees from abusing the system. These efforts are supported by purchasing systems that enable these command-and-control principles.

This puts procurement in a challenging position in terms of building trusting relationships. Too many companies let a few potential bad apples ruin the purchasing experience for everyone, and as a result, procurement loses credibility as a valuable business partner. In the midst of the digital consumer revolution, now is the time to rethink procurement's contribution to the buying process.

Redesigning Procurement with an Eye to the Customer

If you could design a new customer experience for corporate purchasing, what would be the compelling, inspirational North Star to follow? Why not create a buying experience with immediate transparency into prices, shipping options, warranties, and performance reviews so users can make an informed decision? Provide a sleek, fast, and enjoyable experience, but create controls that enable transparency and provide feedback to prevent poor behaviors. Or better yet, use AI to optimize recommendations and provide visibility into supply and demand.

Design the customer experience with a "trust but verify" mindset. In other words, give users flexibility and choices but with the necessary guide rails. This approach also improves procurement's ability to quickly detect fraudulent activities, avoid overpayments, and simplify regulatory compliance. Once the new process is in place, verify and publicize the results to show how procurement is adding value.

This approach will require plotting a new course—much more than simply putting the same cast of characters through a half-day brainstorming session. The consumerization of procurement will require a comprehensive methodology, such as design thinking. Combining design thinking and workshops with procurement end users and IT can shed light on a powerful new approach that identifies issues, uncovers needs, and prioritizes an optimal solution. Inspired by the digital revolution, these new requirements must employ a microservices architecture, best of breed solutions, advanced analytics, and intelligent automation—underpinning the entire solution with a business process management workflow system (see ◘ Fig. 2.2).

Much of Procurement Will Soon Be Automated

Operational procurement is well on its way to becoming fully automated through AI. Major components such as procure-to-pay (P2P) are going in that direction, and so are even higher-value functions, such as automated buying, AI sourcing managers, and chatbot supplier help desks. AI is already embedded in individual applications, including services sourcing, where it guides buyers through supplier identification, the RFP event, and creation of statements of work. The tools empower users, freeing them to buy what they need without procurement's interference. Instead, procurement's value-add is that it engineered the system to deliver a seamless buying experience that fits within the enterprise's strategic objectives.

Similarly, AI can be embedded into predictive supplier-risk monitoring to read nascent signals and proactively take the appropriate action without human intervention. For example, if the system is monitoring a supply base and a supplier

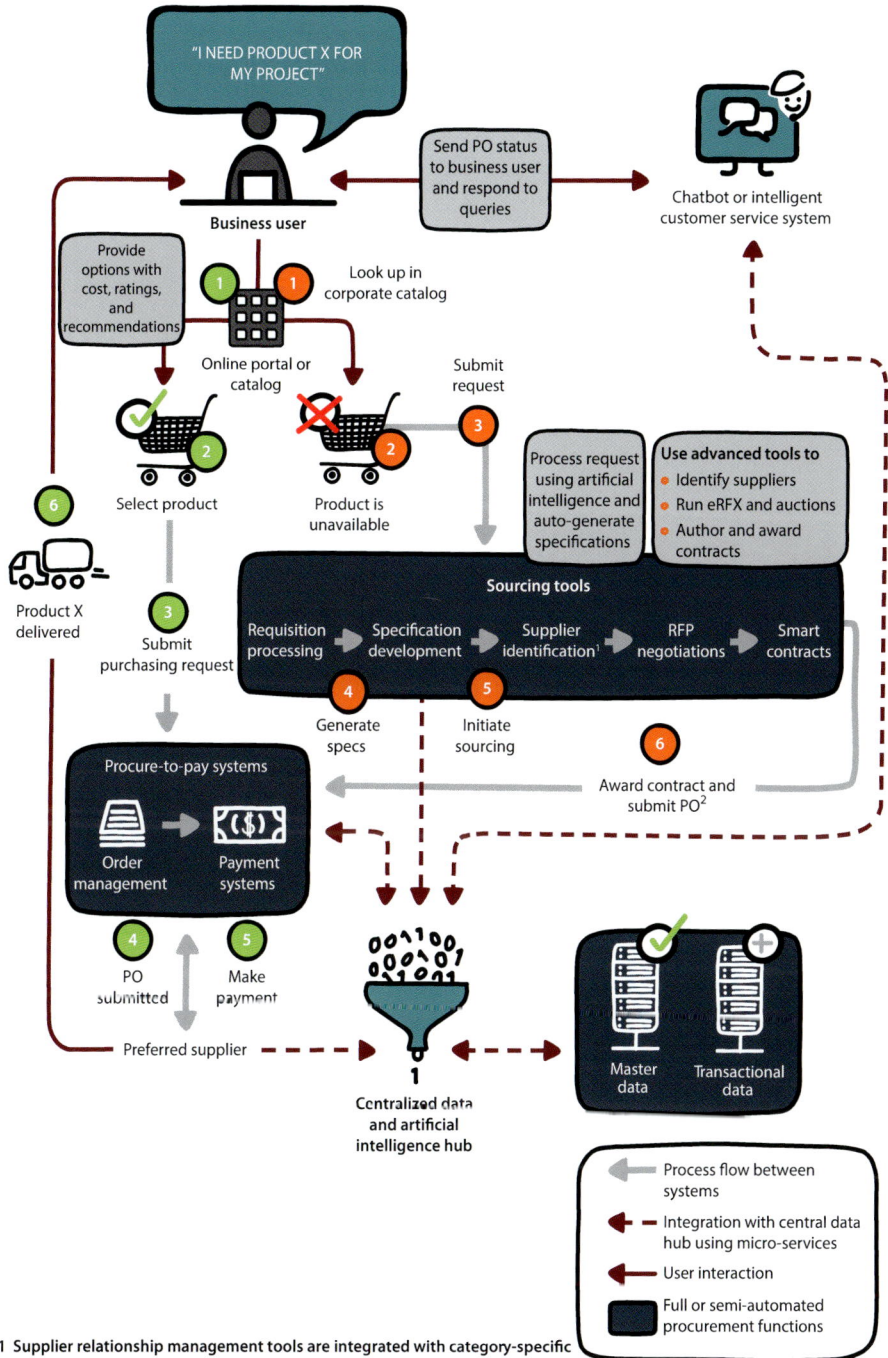

■ Fig. 2.2   What the procurement user experience should be

2

becomes embroiled in a bribery scandal on the other side of the world, the system can automatically score the initial risk, monitor it, adjust the risk score as more information comes in, and pull up all contracts and spend associated with that supplier so that the company can make decisions should the scandal grow. Going further, the AI system could also use natural-language generation to draft and post press releases and social media content to manage the story.

Perhaps the new technology with the greatest potential is blockchain. Smart contracts using blockchain can prevent money from being spent in the wrong place, which would eliminate all the effort in building spend cubes. These contracts can be programmed to monitor supplier performance and reconcile it against the terms and conditions and then dispense payments as conditions are met. Blockchain could condense and redefine the entire contract management and P2P processes. It is important to note that blockchain is still in its infancy and still lacks an agreed-upon underlying technology protocol. However, assuming it comes to fruition, it will change how contracts are negotiated and disrupt the traditional negotiation levers. Forward-looking organizations will see benefits by riding this wave early with an understanding that blockchain will require patience and a significant investment.

Begin the Tech Journey Now

There is no off-the-shelf game plan for adopting these new procurement technologies and architecture. It is a journey that requires a CPO to have vision and passion because technological progress is never easy. Forward-thinking procurement organizations that want to eliminate their aging, underutilized technology assets can choose one of three paths.

- *Make a like-for-like replacement with an updated core source-to-pay (S2P) system.* For example, if a company owns Ariba, switch to Coupa or vice-versa. Taking this path usually requires a couple of years and creates expenditures in the seven-figure range. It is also a one-shot decision where the business is committed to a specific technology for another generation or so.
- *Make a like-for-like replacement and keep the existing system while adopting individual best-of-breed solutions.* This is the least disruptive path. One global company we worked with is taking this route. Knowing that its S2P platform will run out of life within the next couple of years, the company is piloting new tools to manage risk. The expectation is that the company may not implement an all-embracing S2P replacement, but rather a set of agile tools that connect with one another. Many others may need to tackle the dilemma of being left with a white-elephant S2P solution (despite investing millions of dollars) by choosing this option as a way to ease the transition to non-traditional providers and technologies.
- *Embrace the new architecture, and adopt individual solutions, updating them as they evolve.* This route lets companies enjoy the benefits of being a first mover and influence the evolution of these technologies. This is actually the least risky in the long run because it avoids overinvesting in what will rapidly become outdated technology. However, because it will take several years to fully realize the benefits, this route requires having a certain type of CPO who has unique

AS-IS	Blend	Best-of-breed
1. Full-scale replacement with new/upgraded end-to-end procurement suite	2. Full-scale replacement with new/upgraded end-to-end procurement suite and adoption of new technology	3. Agile enhancement of existing procurement technology, integrating and connecting to best-in-class functional specialists

Benefits

AS-IS	Blend	Best-of-breed
• Single end-to-end procurement suite (lower complexity)	• Best-of-breed backend procurement tool, fully customized to user journeys (highest benefits potential) • Agile adoption of new technology, enables short-term benefits	• Modest investment over time and future-proof • Accelerated delivery of benefits • Tools can be chosen to customize the right journeys

Trade-offs

AS-IS	Blend	Best-of-breed
• Significant investment commitment over a 2- to 3-year rollout • Benefits realization takes years as opposed to months	• High level of investment over a 2- to 3-year rollout	• Existing technology backbone remains (over time intelligent and automated technologies may supersede the old systems)

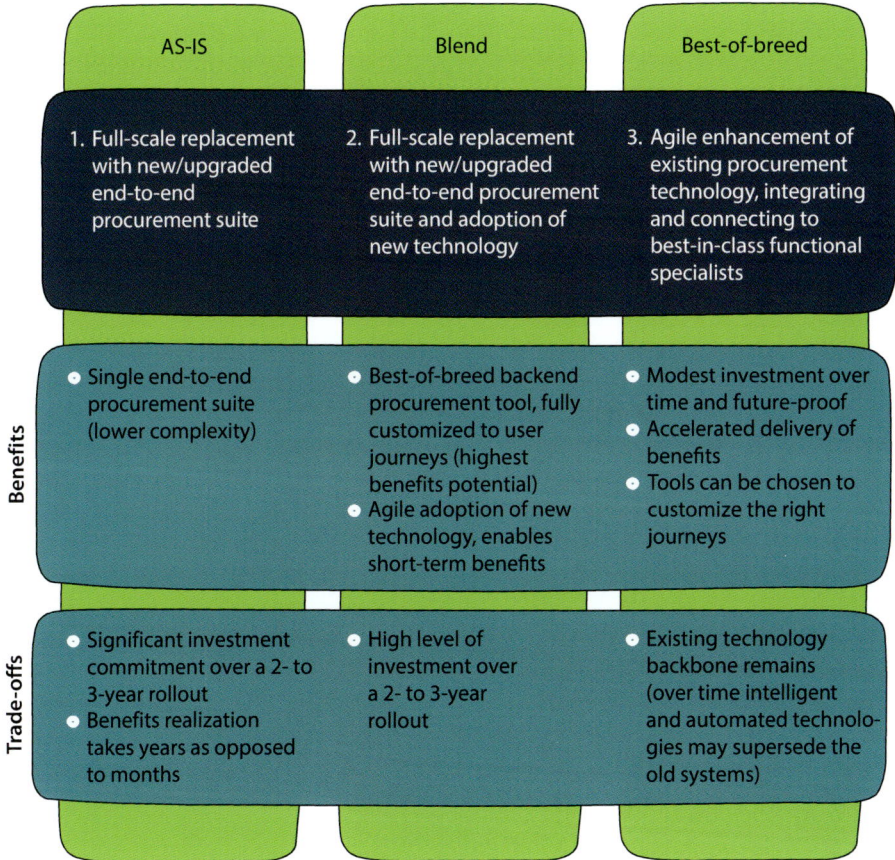

▣ Fig. 2.3 Starting the procurement technology journey

leadership skills—one who is in it for the long haul. We believe, though, that this third option, when paired with significant automation, will be the right answer for more procurement functions (see ▣ Fig. 2.3).

Speed Chess Will Be the Name of the Game

Many of the exciting technological advances will disrupt indirect categories such as marketing or maintenance, where spending tends to be unstructured and fragmented with a myriad of people across functions making purchases. Because many companies still use manual processes for indirect expenditures, technology will radically transform the way these purchases are made.

But when it comes to direct expenditures, technology will not have quite the same impact. Spending on products that are part of the bill of materials tends to be much more structured with clear specifications, costs that are captured in the accounting system to enable inventory valuation, and strong controls.

Technological and macro changes will trigger radical shifts in manufacturing and greater information transparency through digital innovation.

However, these broad changes are coming from beyond procurement—shifting the balance of power between supply and demand. For direct buyers, preparing for and taking advantage of these shifts will be essential. The winners will be those that tackle direct procurement like a strategic game of speed chess.

Supply and demand power is fundamental to direct procurement—determining category strategies, influencing the leverage over supplier behaviors, and playing a role in determining profitability in direct supply chains. Kearney's Purchasing Chessboard® reveals a number of factors that determine power, such as the relative concentration of suppliers and buyers, barriers to entry in the supply market, and substitute products. Over time, two factors regulate the balance of power: suppliers' ability to create and maintain the uniqueness and scarcity that buyers need, and buyers' ability to find alternative ways to meet their needs and challenge suppliers' uniqueness and scarcity. This is a love–hate relationship. Direct suppliers need to perform well to meet their customers' needs, while suppliers may also be selling to the competition. Exclusivity is a chimera that is rarely maintained forever.

In the long run, a variety of players along the supply chain are vying with each other to increase their relative power. The dynamics of this jockeying for position are changing, fueled by macro trends in production automation and information transparency—forces that are coming from beyond the procurement world. The predominant impact is that buyers in most direct markets are becoming more powerful. This shift in business-to-business markets mirrors what is happening in many business-to-consumer markets, where the buyer is king and traditional businesses are being disrupted. These shifts are making their way through the supply chain with a domino effect.

For buyers grappling with inflation and long-term concerns about scarcity and labor-market demographics, this may all seem counterintuitive. However, their relative power along direct supply chains will increase over time. It's important to consider three points:

- *Suppliers' uniqueness and scarcity will be harder to maintain.* Manufacturers will continue to face the disruptive force of technology. Ultrafast 3D printing is one of the most ubiquitous disruptors, but other technologies are emerging, including light-based manufacturing, embedded metrology, and simulation. Wider digital developments also mean that knowledge will be disseminated faster, and the ability to replicate innovative designs in a way that does not infringe copyrights, patent laws, and other forms of intellectual property protection will increase. This is reducing suppliers' ability to create an enduring, inherent uniqueness and scarcity, and intellectual property is becoming harder to keep. Still, suppliers must be able to innovate and improve their performance on cost, quality, and responsiveness. The most successful innovations will target consumers' needs and be co-created with them to ensure the product or service hits the mark.

- *Buyers will find it easier to obtain alternatives.* Suppliers' ability to find and use alternatives from the supply market is growing. The digital tools to find new suppliers are better than ever and can be deployed systematically. Even more importantly, though, the ability to analytically understand specifications is stronger. In the not-too-distant past, buyers had to rely on hand-produced drawings that were hard to analyze and difficult to locate. Better tools to analyze and digitize drawings, break down specifications, and communicate the requirements with a wider supply base are becoming more common.

Product teardowns are also becoming more systematized, enabling buyers to challenge specifications and open new supply markets with product redesigns. For example, in teardown labs, industrial engineers and associated experts disassemble products to identify the individual components. The list of components then enables a company to develop fact-based insights into the quality, materials, and processes that competitors are using to make their products or particular elements of the company's own products. These lists can then be used to lower costs, rationalize a portfolio, or pursue new opportunities. This can be done, for example, by optimizing the mix of ingredients to reduce costs, based on commodity pricing or changing packaging to improve the package-to-product ratio. As a result, buyers are gaining power. The crucial question is whether they can wield this power and take advantage of the alternatives.

- *Although the impact will not be uniform across supply chains, the direction of travel is clear.* Suppliers' power will endure in some areas, especially if they have preferential access to prime commodities that are both desired and in short supply. However, the forces of innovation will be disruptive. For example, because mined diamonds have come under intense scrutiny by regulators as well as social responsibility activists, companies are being challenged to use synthetic alternatives in industrial applications as well as for consumer use.

Other industries may be more reluctant to embrace new alternatives and take perceived risks that will challenge the status quo in the supply market. For example, the aerospace industry has long product lifecycles and is highly risk-averse given the overwhelming need to put safety first. Incumbent suppliers will retain a large degree of power, based on the stickiness of buyers and the challenges of replicating a suppliers' intellectual property. Much of the supplier uniqueness is based on custom and practice know-how that is hard to systematize and scale easily in a world of low-volume manufacturing.

Contrast this with the high-tech industry, where multiple generations of products are launched within the lifetime of one airframe or engine. High volume in high tech also enables a more systematized approach in which suppliers can be commoditized more easily, unless they innovate and improve performance. Yet even the aerospace industry is changing as it converges with the high-tech industry. Suppliers' ability to retain residual power will be greater here than in many other faster-moving and less risk-averse sectors.

Other factors will also affect the speed of change. For example, tariffs and other government restrictions may enable some suppliers to insulate themselves for a time. Rules that seek to limit the ability to recreate intellectual property may also be involved. These will delay but not change the underlying domino effect as buyers' power increases across the supply chain (see ◘ Fig. 2.4).

2

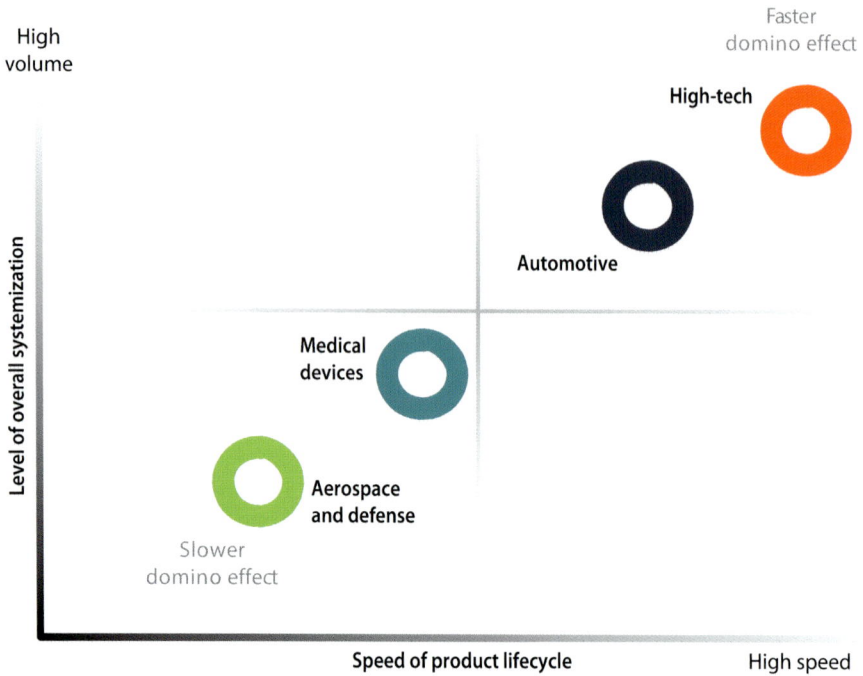

Fig. 2.4   More power for buyers in high-volume industries with fast product lifecycles

Suppliers Will Not Surrender

Constant improvement and innovation are the only mantras for suppliers' long-term success.

Although erecting walls as impediments will not be a sustainable option, this will not stop many suppliers from trying to do just that. In fact, many will try to resist the reduction in relative power. Some will attempt to move upstream to get closer to scarce commodities that they hope to control, and some will seek artificial ways to keep power by using tariffs, regulations, and restrictions on using intellectual property.

Many manufacturers have already moved into providing services associated with their products, such as maintenance, outsourced machine operations, and even selling their data as a product. The growing ubiquity of digital and the IoT means that data is a competitive weapon. This has increased supplier power by making buyers less keen to switch and appears to be part of a response to manufacturing becoming less unique. Expect to see more suppliers going down this path—inflating the value of the services and data they provide as a way to create stickiness.

Buyers Need a Ruthless Focus on Gaining Power and Using It

In the future, buyers' overall power will increase, but an individual buyer's decisions will affect the degree to which he or she can gain power and then use it. This will require playing a long-term game to capture relative power. At the same time, buyers will need to be nimble to take advantage of new opportunities—seeking alternatives while never losing sight of the big picture.

There are three practical ways to do this:

- *Retain open choices.* As much as possible, remain unconstrained in the supply market. Be prepared to sacrifice short-term gains at the expense of the long-term ability to retain free decision making. Also, seek to avoid lock-ins with suppliers as part of a multi-year approach.
- *Strategically manage intellectual property.* Retain or take control of the intellectual property needed to wield power in the supply market and compete in the product market. Be especially careful with respect to design rights and ownership of drawings, specs and data. Avoid suspending commercial judgment and getting carried away with the strategic relationship.
- *Make use of supplier innovation.* Consider the alternatives and develop ways to improve your competitiveness by taking advantage of supplier-driven innovation. Invest in suppliers that can bring game-changing innovations. Be prepared to create exclusive supply agreements with vendors but maintain control of the intellectual property that creates a competitive advantage.

These recommendations are in line with today's best practices for direct procurement. And yet, buyers will need to be far more agile in how they deploy the techniques to take advantage of the opportunities and the domino effect of buyers' escalating power. The Purchasing Chessboard® will still be relevant, but it will need to be deployed on steroids—like a tactical round of speed chess.

Apple Has Already Made the Next Move

In many ways, the high-tech industry is already pointing to the future of direct procurement. Apple is a good example, having used its supply chain to create a huge competitive advantage. A significant part of the iPad's success can be traced to the exclusivity arrangement the company created with Corning's Gorilla Glass before the product became a blockbuster. This left competitors years behind in the tablet market and is a classic example of leveraging supplier innovation in a smart way.

Apple also invests in constructing supplier factories to manufacture components such as touchscreens, chips, and LED displays. In return, Apple receives exclusive rights to the products that those factories produce, keeping competitors at bay by deterring access to these essential assets. And all the while, Apple can charge a premium for its products. When competitors eventually catch up, Apple is ahead of the game—producing the product cheaper and capturing more profits. Then, the cycle starts again in a process of constant innovation in manufacturing, design and process, where no members of the supply chain can erect permanent walls to protect their position but must constantly improve.

Apple does not appear to be sentimental about these arrangements and avoids getting locked into supplier relationships. Relative demand and supply power are managed, as is the key intellectual property needed to compete. The recent dispute between Apple and Imagination Technologies is a good example. Imagination was a long-standing supplier of technology for the graphics processing units in Apple's mobile devices. This intellectual property is obviously essential, and Apple has developed its own technology, ending its use of Imagination's technology. This business-focused and unsentimental behavior is a prime example of pursuing open choices and managing key intellectual property. This approach is not all that surprising, given that Apple CEO Tim Cook has a background as a supply chain leader.

The core skills and tools of direct procurement will become more pertinent than ever, as buyers gain power. Businesses and their buyers that can master these will have a strong competitive advantage. However, the industry is facing a talent shortage.

Procurement Talent: It's Time to Panic

With automation quickly making today's skills irrelevant, the days of procurement staff as order-takers is over. The skills required to do the job today—haggling, monitoring, and executing tasks—will become irrelevant as automation makes these basic tasks unnecessary. With the rise of robotic process automation and cognitive AI, transactional work such as placing orders is rapidly disappearing. And yet, top-quality talent is a scarce commodity.

Eventually, more complex work such as indirect category management will also vanish. An organization with 1,000 employees today will likely have 100 in the not-too-distant future—and those that survive will have a much different set of skills.

Beyond procurement, most enterprises are engaging in some sort of digital transformation that is rationalizing legacy jobs (especially back-office jobs), reengineering and streamlining processes to drive efficiency, and looking to hire talent with twenty-first-century skills, such as analytics fluency, design thinking and agility. Simultaneously, technology companies, startups, and even non-profits are attracting those with great skills and even greater potential: Gen Y employees. Unlike their Millennial predecessors, Gen Y employees have spent their entire lives immersed in sophisticated technologies such as AI, big data, programming, and on-demand access to top-notch educational content online. However, while this generation and those that follow will eventually become ubiquitous in the employment market, there are only so many of these people available today. Thus, it is a classic problem of supply and demand: there is a finite supply of talent amid massive demand. This dynamic is complicated by the fact that, in addition to commercial success, many in Gen Y seek altruism and a true sense of social value.

Making matters more complex is the fact that the benefits of acquiring and cultivating talent are long-term at best. This is challenging in an era where there is more pressure to drive immediate and significant results. Any CPO investing in talent may not be around to reap the rewards or receive the credit for his or her efforts. In fact, any time and money spent on talent today may impinge on short-term benefits. Yet doing nothing is not an option either, because large low-value organizations are already under pressure to downsize and reduce costs. So those that value the profession and the long-term success of the business will choose this despite the lack of obvious short-term payoff.

New Skills and a Whole-Brain Approach

Procurement of the future must proactively provide high-quality customer-focused experiences—a by-product of the digital consumer revolution. In practical terms, this means locating procurement with the product lines so they can anticipate and respond rapidly. This also requires deployment of critical skills, which are not mutually exclusive, in support of the required new areas of focus:

- *Overall process orchestration.* Building and sustaining customer-focused experiences requires abilities such as design thinking, process engineering, complex vendor management and fluency in technology architectures.
- *Strategic category management.* Managing supply-and-demand power requires left-brain traits, such as logic, reasoning, numbers, and analytical thinking, which are crucial for value-added activities such as total lifecycle management, value-based sourcing, and collaborative cost reduction.
- *Supplier relationship management.* Advanced supplier relationship management (SRM) requires right-brain traits, such as creativity, intuition, emotional intelligence, and visual comprehension, which are crucial to accomplishing initiatives such as strategic alliances, supplier development, and sustainability innovation. It also requires advanced negotiation skills that go far beyond classic haggling techniques.

Moreover, employees will need to embrace often-overlooked skills such as written and verbal communication, listening, and personal reputation management and branding (see ◘ Fig. 2.5). Communication skills in particular will require being adept at making clear and concise arguments as well as writing in both long- and short-form narratives. Procurement personnel must be comfortable presenting to a wide variety of audiences from the board and executive level to hundreds of general business users. In short, they will need to be good storytellers—both written and verbal—to convey the relevant business cases, benefits and value-creation components.

Procurement Is Beginning to Look Like a Tech Company

Successful tech companies treat their services and solutions as products, and they employ product managers—or at least have a product manager mindset. Product managers own a solution from end to end—from development and deployment to usage and ongoing enhancement. Colloquially, product managers are often referred to as a product CEO.

2

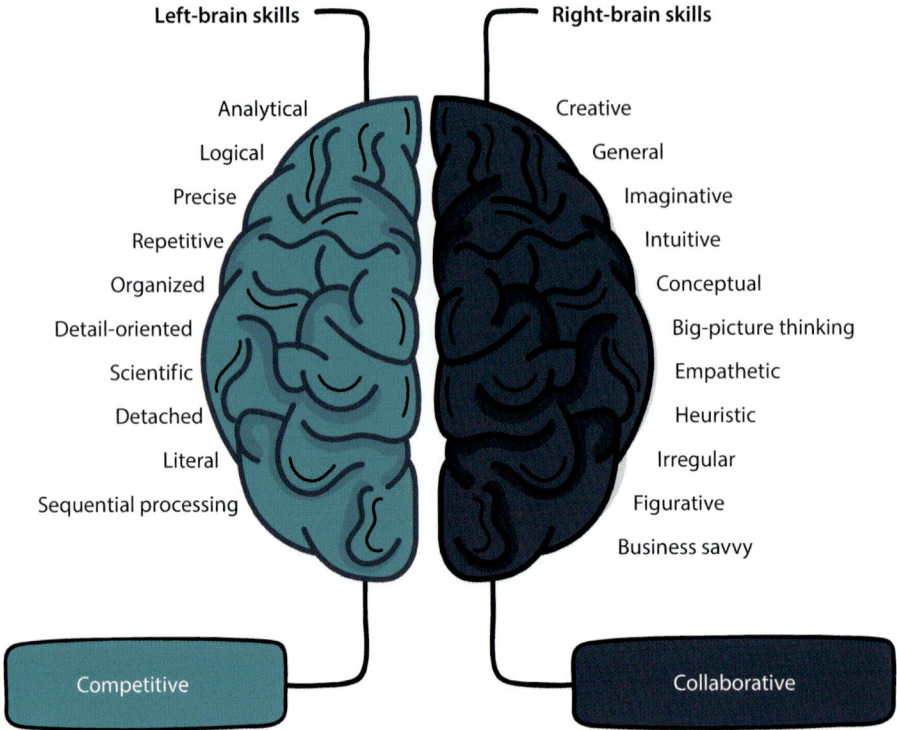

Left-brain skills	Right-brain skills
Analytical	Creative
Logical	General
Precise	Imaginative
Repetitive	Intuitive
Organized	Conceptual
Detail-oriented	Big-picture thinking
Scientific	Empathetic
Detached	Heuristic
Literal	Irregular
Sequential processing	Figurative
	Business savvy
Competitive	Collaborative

☐ **Fig. 2.5** Procurement thinking – whole-brain thinking

At any point, they can articulate the current or projected return on investment, areas for improvement, and level of customer satisfaction. This ensures full accountability and transparency and creates the best opportunities for customer satisfaction, which can then be measured at the individual, organizational and executive levels. Effective product managers are curious and passionate about how their solutions are being used. They continually invent solutions to problems, innovate new features, and simplify processes. Leaders empower these product managers to be nimble, take risks, and make decisions that support the business needs.

Successful tech companies also continuously measure customer satisfaction by using net promoter scores to quantify whether a product or service is meeting users' needs. This requires soliciting user feedback and turning it into practical insights, a process that needs checking one's ego at the door. Simply sending a survey is nowhere near good enough. Successful product managers try to grasp what silent users are doing, knowing that they are often the ones who are too frustrated to engage in a constructive dialog to improve the product or service. In these cases, product managers must double down on behavioral analytics to predict, test and validate improvements.

As procurement starts to operate more like a tech company, it will become more attractive to the new generation of talent. As other functions struggle for identity and relevance in the age of automation, procurement will benefit. For example, who would want to go into accounting when bots will streamline—and eviscerate—the function? However, procurement can use the same automation techniques to offload low-value tasks to pursue more strategic, impactful, and socially conscious ways to help the business and society. That will surely be appealing to many.

Get Moving—You're Already Late

There is no time to waste. Given the finite supply, the competition for talent is a no-holds-barred affair. Perhaps the most important step will be rebranding. Historically, procurement has had an image problem. The idea of haggling with suppliers and enforcing purchasing controls appealed to few. Consequently, procurement struggled to attract and retain the best talent. Yet, in an era where procurement can drive innovation with suppliers, use cutting-edge technology such as negotiation bots, and implement a true sustainability program, this traditionally dowdy function suddenly looks a whole lot more appealing.

Rebranding itself is not some fake exercise where everyone sits in a room thinking of adjectives to describe the group. It should be a fundamental mindset revolution paired with an attitude adjustment that shifts the focus to the excitement and social difference procurement can make. These are messages that will resonate with the Millennials and Gen Y.

Because people with these advanced skills are not easy to find, companies will have to work doubly hard to build a robust pipeline of talent. This is not a passive activity. CPOs and leaders will need to hustle to win out over not only startups and other competitors, but also other groups within the same enterprise. This means having an active presence at universities with programs that equip students with the right mix of skills and experience. Doing lectures, sponsoring theses, and recruiting are just a few of the many ways to engage with—and inspire—the next generation.

Unfortunately, there is no obvious roadmap for engaging with universities. For a long time now, procurement organizations have had an eclectic composition of talent, with people taking all manners of journeys to get there. And there are no procurement feeder schools like there are for finance, IT, and other more traditional disciplines. Few graduate programs exist for procurement, and there are even fewer at the undergraduate level. Although there is nothing wrong with an eclectic approach to team-building, procurement is at a disadvantage because there is no central talent pool from which to draw. Ambitious leaders will see this as an opportunity to build custom university partnerships and have first pick at new talent.

In addition to looking externally for talent, there are likely rough stones in the internal employee pool that can be polished into diamonds. If there are 1,000 employees today, statistically speaking, a portion of them should have some of the skills and desire to make the transition to the new paradigm. This will require doing a multi-level capability and character assessment. Investing in employees who make the cut and can make the transition will pay huge dividends.

2

Ultimately, procurement is exciting, and the CPO and his or her leadership must convey a sense of excitement. The ability to create a buzz around procurement will provide an advantage in the push for talent. Creating excitement can be easy, as good procurement makes a difference, not only to the bottom line, but also to society. Tracking and contracting suppliers with sustainable practices or socially conscious agendas, or helping them to adopt these behaviors, sits squarely within procurement's purview. For upwardly mobile employees who aspire to leadership positions in other disciplines, procurement is an excellent place to advance from for roles beyond procurement. What better place to learn how an organization operates than to engage in its supply base and external spend? And procurement done well will give tomorrow's leaders the necessary hands-on experience in strategy for CEO and other senior leadership roles.

Procurement of the future will focus on its true reason for being: how it can translate supply market value into product value. Doing this effectively will require a new operating model and more advanced capabilities.

Today, detailed procurement operating models (and the scope of the function itself) vary across industry and within industries based on many factors. Nevertheless, most are center-led and category-focused, with allowances made for specific geographies for local categories and for enabling user engagement. Often, a back-office processing function takes care of simple tactical sourcing needs and administration of procure-to-pay systems.

Procurement of the future will align to product-customer offer teams to shape categories that directly impact the product offer, with a focus on high-value commercial input and orchestration of supplier behavior. For other categories of spend, the focus will be on user enablement and automation, recognizing that users want to purchase solutions that may cut across classic categories. The categories that directly impact the product offer will vary by business and industry. Typically, all direct categories impact the product and, depending on the situation, a proportion of the indirect ones. The traditional accounting-driven, direct–indirect split is not necessarily helpful in this respect (see ◘ Fig. 2.6).

A Procurement Imperative for CEOs

During a company's day-to-day operations, procurement is often low on the agenda, even though the function is essential to financial performance. In fact, depending on the industry, external spending can be more than half of a company's overall cost base. World-class procurement is about much more than delivering savings from better deals with suppliers. A CPO's true objective is to improve the competitiveness of the business by converting supply market value into product value. This must be of deep interest to CEOs, and in the future, doing this well will be increasingly important for a company's competitiveness.

These moves can ensure procurement is creating the most value:

- Drive bottom-line improvements with strategic sourcing that addresses supplier choices, specifications, service levels and systematic demand management. This includes robust approaches to ensure that financial benefits land directly in the income statement rather than being frittered away or getting lost.

Categories integral to the product offer

- Varies by industry but usually includes all direct, packaging, marketing, and other spend that directly impacts the offer
- Operating model aligned to products
- Procurement activity integrated in product development or innovation teams to improve the offer

Procurement role predominantly

- Providing high-value commercial input—orchestrating supply and demand power
- Obtaining the right behavior from suppliers—managing relationships well

Categories not integral to the product offer

- Varies by industry but usually includes most indirect categories including facilities, professionals services, repairs, transport, and IT
- Operating model aligned to user communities
- Procurement activity focused on supporting users to buy solutions to meet their needs

Procurement role predominantly

- Ensuring technological enablement is in place—so that users or stakeholders can self-serve as much as possible
- End-to-end orchestration—ensuring that the processes and enablement work, including the data analytics to make decisions

Fig. 2.6 New procurement operating model

- Create the right supplier behaviors to achieve the organization's objectives for innovation, sustainability and risk management, as well as creating winning ecosystems across the supply market.
- Manage supplier interactions in a differentiated way according to the value the supplier can bring and deploy it across the whole organization.

2

- Make the purchasing experience straightforward for internal users so they can focus on their core roles.
- Orchestrate the end-to-end user specify-to-pay process so transacting with suppliers is seamless, effective and efficient across the organization while still being controlled.

Only a small number of global leaders achieve these outcomes. This approach can bring above-normal financial benefits as seen in Kearney's Assessment of Excellence in Procurement (AEP) studies over the past three decades—to the tune of a 60 percent higher return over and above the cost of running procurement, compared with what is typically achieved by non-leader procurement functions. Leaders sustain this result over time—even after a merger.[1]

The CEO–CPO Disconnect

The first step is to understand the common misalignments between CEOs and CPOs. CEOs typically have several needs from the external market, predominantly bottom-line improvements to enhance profits with sustainable cost reduction, as well as innovation to help grow the top line while also managing risk. In addition, many CEOs want to know how well procurement is performing compared with the competition, and they want to translate supply market value into product value.

Although no CPO would disagree with any of these needs, procurement often doesn't tackle these points head on. Procurement's focus is often on savings, commercials, and legal remedies. There is nothing wrong with any of these objectives; they simply do not go far enough, which can frustrate CEOs.

In that respect, savings are usually the prime currency that procurement uses to measure its contribution to the bottom line. Many CEOs often rightly distrust claims about savings and, of course, want to enhance profits. They also intuitively understand that measuring savings is not an exact science. CPOs then spend much of their energy discussing savings that do not always affect the bottom line and that they cannot fully control anyway. Then, they lack the authority needed to control the end-to-end processes to do their job effectively, including procure-to-pay processes to lock in savings. This includes offering an effective service to users and overall orchestration of supplier relationship management to ensure that the commercial perspective is considered in all supplier interactions. Instead, they end up conceding authority for these processes (often implicitly) to other CxOs who have different objectives.

The processes that CPOs do control then often become administrative tasks that slow users down rather than create value with better specifications, more

---

1   For more information, see ▶ https://www.kearney.com/procurement/the-assessment-of-excellence-in-procurement-study

suitable supplier choices, and fit-for-purpose commercial terms. By pursuing this course, CPOs can create undue drama that makes them look bad to the CEO and C-suite. The primary business objectives of delivering innovation from the supply base and managing risk then get overlooked and are not tackled systematically. There is even a tendency to assume that other functions will launch the capabilities that procurement needs. For example, one global CPO told us it was not his job to build an analytics capability. In another organization, finance controlled the process of giving spend information to procurement—rationing it and adorning it with accounting policy-related add-ons that clouded transparency into what had been spent when and with whom.

It's easy to see why many CEOs think procurement is only about making deals and haggling with suppliers with a limited focus on translating supply market value into product value. Many question procurement's claims about its value and get frustrated that they lack a yardstick to measure the results of their procurement compared with their competitors (see ◘ Fig. 2.7).

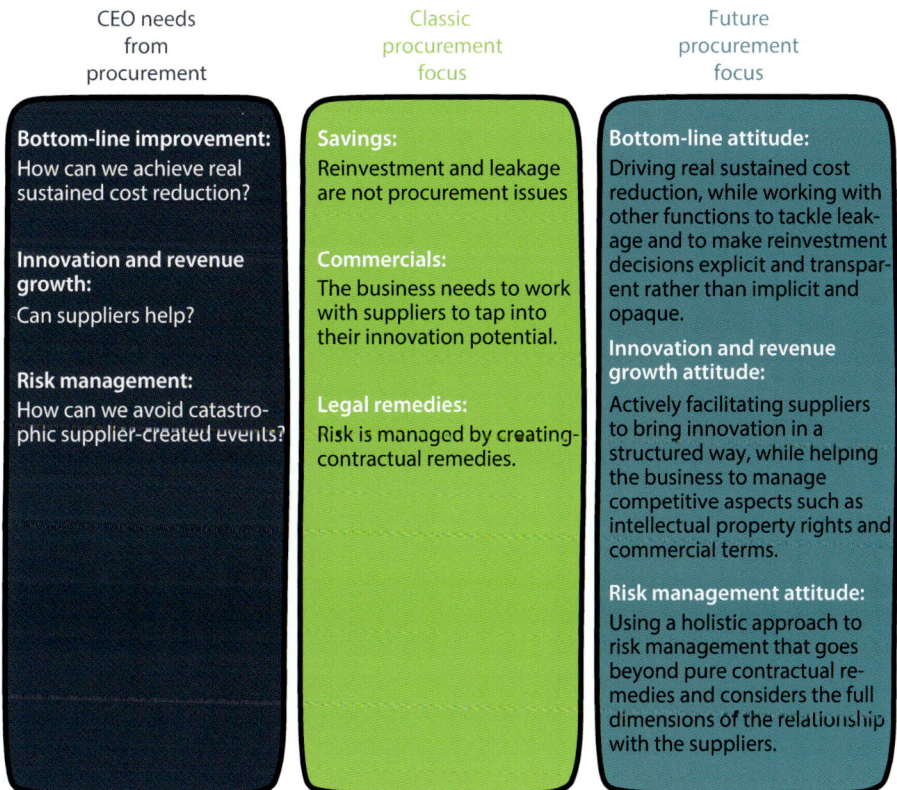

CEO needs from procurement	Classic procurement focus	Future procurement focus
Bottom-line improvement: How can we achieve real sustained cost reduction?	**Savings:** Reinvestment and leakage are not procurement issues	**Bottom-line attitude:** Driving real sustained cost reduction, while working with other functions to tackle leakage and to make reinvestment decisions explicit and transparent rather than implicit and opaque.
Innovation and revenue growth: Can suppliers help?	**Commercials:** The business needs to work with suppliers to tap into their innovation potential.	**Innovation and revenue growth attitude:** Actively facilitating suppliers to bring innovation in a structured way, while helping the business to manage competitive aspects such as intellectual property rights and commercial terms.
Risk management: How can we avoid catastrophic supplier-created events?	**Legal remedies:** Risk is managed by creating contractual remedies.	**Risk management attitude:** Using a holistic approach to risk management that goes beyond pure contractual remedies and considers the full dimensions of the relationship with the suppliers.

◘ **Fig. 2.7** CEOs and CPOs – often out of alignment

2

If procurement is not effective, then value is being left on the table. Many CPOs need to be more ambitious, take more internal risks and communicate the value they can bring. To do this, they need CEOs who encourage and nurture their role. That raises the question: How can CEOs create an environment that values procurement so the company can reap the benefits?

How CEOs Can Support CPOs

As mentioned, leading procurement organizations deliver 60 percent higher returns on the assets invested in procurement—with significant benefits to the bottom line beyond the added value of addressing supplier behavior and reducing supply chain risks. In these companies, the CPO is a senior member of the executive team who can be trusted and held accountable for articulating and executing the function's agenda.

There are three practical ways for a CEO to set up a CPO for success.

Agree to a Center-Led Operating Model

A center-led operating model is crucial for effective procurement. The procurement team needs to report to the CPO, who then needs to be able to deploy the team on the most value-adding activities and have accountability for achieving results. This way of operating creates a wealth of opportunities to deploy best-practice processes, build professional capability across the function, and drive the widest possible value from external spend.

However, this needs to be done in a way that avoids a silo mentality. There are many examples of centralized procurement functions that end up disconnected from the business, creating strategies that do not land with stakeholders even though they looked good from a procurement perspective. Instead of creating value, this approach can result in the edifice later being dismantled and the pendulum swinging back to a decentralized model. Leading CPOs deploy the model in a way that considers a variety of stakeholders' needs and provides a service to the business rather than dictating outcomes. A supportive CEO encourages the center-led approach while stressing the need for balanced governance to ensure procurement does not become all-powerful in a counterproductive way.

Support CPO Ownership of Value-Creating Processes

In leading organizations, the CPO owns the core value-added processes required for effective procurement, including the strategic sourcing process for selecting suppliers, agreeing on specifications and service levels, and creating policies for managing demand. This does not necessarily mean CPOs make all the decisions, but they are responsible for deploying strategic sourcing and guiding the business to achieve the right outcomes. They have the power to consider new approaches and are responsible for all external expenditures.

However, many organizations make exceptions to this approach. For example, some chief marketing officers have the power to say that spending on above-the-line and below-the-line marketing is outside the scope of procurement because it has unique drivers. And for banks, some categories such as market data are also considered to be beyond procurement's jurisdiction.

This should not be allowed. Typically, earmarking an expenditure area as being out of scope is a mask for non-value-added practices, incumbent suppliers that have not been challenged for a long time, and out-of-date approaches to specifying requirements and setting demand levels. CPOs need to make their own case, win the right to be involved and argue for their own corner. In leading companies, the CEO understands that all external expenditures should be the domain of procurement and is prepared to help the CPO defend this with any reluctant colleagues.

Similarly, the CPO needs to own the supplier relationship management process to obtain the right supplier behaviors and manage risk by measuring and giving feedback about supplier performance as well as ensuring contract and service level compliance. This includes working with selected strategic suppliers to capitalize on their potential to bring innovation to the business that can fuel competitive performance. The CPO should not own all resources involved in supplier management since business stakeholders are often closest to the issues associated with specific suppliers and contracts. However, the CPO needs to deploy the overall process that others will follow and ensure that the commercial perspective is brought in appropriately during all dealings with suppliers.

Procure-to-pay is the final piece of the procurement process, enabling users to make purchases against pre-agreed contracts and enabling suppliers to be paid. Procurement needs to own this process, too. Again, this does not need to include all resources. For example, requirements for segregating duties often mean that the staff of accounts payable report to the CFO. But the ability to steer procure-to-pay is fundamental to delivering the most value from procurement and for creating an efficient and effective user experience. The front end of the process is how users are routed to the right pre-sourced suppliers with the right specifications, or guided to seek the right help, if a new agreement is needed. The back end of the process in payables gives transparency into what is spent with whom to aid decision-making. Control of these areas is necessary to enable procurement to improve the bottom line.

Create Shared Comprehensive Targets for Procurement

Procurement cannot deliver value in isolation. Real value comes from factors such as a willingness to choose different suppliers, the use of different specifications and service levels, and systematically managing demand. Benefits are only realized if people use the negotiated deals and avoid doing their own thing.

CPOs should drive the value creation, but if they are the only executive targeted to achieve benefits from external spend, then procurement will not get the support it needs. Therefore, CEOs should ensure targets are shared across the organization to facilitate cross-functional working rather than silos. Procurement then needs to be targeted on a balanced scorecard that includes objectives for financial benefits, quality, innovation, and responsiveness, to ensure the right trade-offs are made.

By the same token, procurement targets need to be comprehensive. Some organizations only allow procurement to claim benefits from pure price reductions for the exact same specification—excluding any benefits from specification and service-level changes, product substitutions, or policy-driven demand reductions. This is counterproductive and does not encourage collaboration or an expansive approach to driving procurement value. Leading organizations allow procurement to create value in all ways—with the stipulation that the benefits get locked into the business so that savings are not just spent.

A Future-Proof Approach

A few global businesses are set up with a future-proof approach. They have consistently achieved double-digit top-line growth, a double-digit net profit margin, and sustained cost reduction while having a highly capable CPO who is part of the top executive team.

In these businesses, procurement is center-led and has ownership of the main value-adding processes along with being a hub for innovation. The benefits created by procurement are comprehensive and go far beyond pure deal-making to embrace new approaches to the supply market, support the company's sustainability agenda, and promote radical process automation. An end-to-end external spend governance approach interlocks procurement benefits into budgets and avoids leakage.

The CPO recruits the best talent from business schools, and working in the procurement function is seen as a career training ground for other roles in the organization. The CEO, CPO and wider executive team have collaborated to create a culture that is highly conducive to great procurement and delivers consistent value year after year.

At these organizations, procurement is not a defensive mindset but rather an offensive weapon that has created exclusive arrangements with ecosystem partners to take advantage of new technology to improve the bottom line and enable sustainability in the supply chain. It has also innovated new economic and sustainable uses of by-products rather than simply negotiating a cheap price for disposal. Procurement has been in the foreground—making things happen and taking value creation to a whole new level.

This level of performance should be the norm. After all, in most organizations, procurement is the corporate-wide function with the strongest orientation toward value creation. Its reach is both broad and deep while still being tangible, practical, and operational—a much different model than, for example, finance, which is focused on the numbers in the accounts.

Procurement done well creates value that no other function can surpass. This is the model to emulate.

Digital in Procurement

Contents

© Springer Nature Switzerland AG 2020
M. F. Strohmer et al., *Disruptive Procurement*, https://doi.org/10.1007/978-3-030-38950-5_3

The Journey to Digital Procurement

Digital procurement is helping companies become more effective and efficient with both strategic and operational procurement. These are important advances that will help procurement take a seat next to the C-suite. With the right digital tools in place for the right processes, procurement can focus on the work that adds value and makes procurement a true strategic partner in the company.

Delivering more added value means going over and beyond procurement's traditional role as cost saver. When procurement is serving as a business partner, it provides insight about potential growth areas, as well as support with optimal pricing and predictive pricing, to name a few examples. In the past, it was procurement's job to discuss historical prices and what had happened in the business. That time is over. Procurement is now about looking forward. As one CPO said: "We cannot go full speed on the motorway looking into the rear-view mirror. We have done that too long."

Companies that lead in procurement bring procurement into business decisions early on. This may include involvement in demand planning, large-scale CAPEX projects, or developing raw material strategies. Procurement professionals have learned not to wait until actual demand arises to begin developing strategies for demand. They are moving ahead and anticipating this demand through the understanding they have gained from new tools and relationships. But procurement's mandate should be even broader: Procurement needs to be a trend scout in the market to drive innovation.

This means using its understanding of the business and of the procurement process to actively scout for new ideas, products and services on the supplier market that could improve a current product or service, or become the basis for a new one. In the past, sales were of utmost importance to companies for achieving growth; today, since speed-to-market is critical, procurement, in its role as an innovation-spotter, may become equally valuable, or even more valuable, for boosting growth.

Procurement needs to be seen as an active partner in business areas such as R&D, marketing and manufacturing. It needs to consider the entire supply and value chain and have an opinion on how the future of particular products and services, as well as customer demand, will shape up. Procurement can do all this because it is equipped with new digital tools that allow for faster access to data, better and faster analyses, and more data via information hubs.

Procurement can shed its image of bureaucracy and use its foresight to help the company avoid apparent and hidden risks. Don't be surprised if procurement offices start to look like control centers, with teams of people monitoring dashboards of indicators that provide a clearer picture of what's happening in the business and what could happen.

In general, procurement should be seen as a center for value creation and a key player in managing enterprise risk.

But getting procurement to this point of maturity – which only a few companies have achieved – means a fundamental change in the organization that involves new capabilities – and new thinking.

3

It's Urgent: Why Procurement Needs to Be Digital Right Now

Making procurement processes more digital and automated, and enabling the organization with tools, is not new to procurement departments. Indeed, the function has a long history of trying to find and adopt new tools and technologies. It is accustomed to handling large sets of data (spend data and specification data, for example) and automating processes.

Companies have been automating the procure-to-pay process since the mid-1990s, and e-auction tools such as Techpilot have been available since then, too. Procurement also has experience in managing complex networks, such as multi-tiered supply bases and internal stakeholder networks, and in implementing digital tools. Now, however, the amount of computing power available has increased significantly, and the speed at which tools are developed is far greater than in the past. With these tools, companies can reduce costs and support innovation, which will develop into a competitive advantage. In addition, there's a stronger focus on digital tools in all areas of business, and implementing them has become a priority in most companies.

While digital tools have long been used for operational procurement, companies now have to implement tools at a faster pace or risk falling behind competitors who do. For example, robotic process automation (RPA) in procurement can reduce data processing time by up to 70 percent, free up to 50 percent of the current procurement workforce, and help reduce material costs by up to an average of 20 percent across categories by 2025, according to Kearney research and project experience. These potential gains make it clear that procurement's strategic value depends on digital tools, and levels of digitalization. Kearney research shows that digital procurement is a top priority for executives; what will differentiate procurement leaders from the laggards is how and when they go about implementing digital tools.

The Impact of Digital on the House of Purchasing and Supply

Digital tools can boost the efficiency and effectiveness of operational and strategic procurement. Efficiency means doing things in an optimal way, with the right balance of time, effort and resources involved, whereas effectiveness means selecting the right things to do and doing them well.

To gain efficiency, many companies seek to automate processes so that procurement can do its job faster and more accurately than in the past. Digital tools for operational procurement are intelligent workload distribution systems, self-service portals, RPA, and process industrialization, for example. RPA can fully automate highly standardized processes and operates about 20 times faster than humans.

To improve procurement effectiveness, companies need to get valuable internal and external data that will help procurement work with deeper understanding and insight to make quicker and better decisions. They also need tools such as predictive analytics, self-learning systems, AI, collaboration platforms, and digital product teardowns, to name a few.

In short, gaining efficiency in procurement will come down to improving processes with digital technologies, advanced tools and in ecosystems. Gaining effectiveness, on the other hand, is about doing completely new things with digital tools and having a strategic impact on the business, based on advanced analytics. If companies make strides in both areas, they can build a powerful procurement function.

For Kearney, the procurement function is built on three core areas that can be further detailed in eight dimensions, as can be seen in ◘ Fig. 3.1. It shows The House of Purchasing and Supply, which was developed in the early 1990s. The Kearney House of Purchasing and Supply is seen as an industry standard framework. Its structure will not change with digitalization, but applications will. Here is an overview of the House of Purchasing and Supply. Later we go into more detail about various tools and technologies and their impact on procurement.

- *Procurement Strategy & Organization (the roof):* Procurement organizations need a clear strategy in place that is fully aligned with the corporate strategy. Executives should define the most important goals, such as savings, higher service levels for the organization, or becoming more innovative. A procurement department that is focused on achieving high savings will invest in different digital tools than those that have made innovation the focus. The strategy should also detail the role of company partners in achieving the stated goals. As digital becomes the norm, we will see a transformation in how procurement organizations are set up and operate – from a pooling of procurement resources to working in sprints.
- *Core Processes (the middle of the House):* The second crucial area consists of three dimensions which will change dramatically with digital procurement:
  - *Sourcing & Category Management:* Some companies struggle to define the right criteria for their desired supply-demand situation. Therefore, Kearney developed the Purchasing Chessboard®, a framework with 64 levers to reduce costs and increase value with suppliers.
  - *Supplier Relationship Management (SRM):* Leading companies define Supplier Interaction Models with their suppliers, in addition to conducting supplier evaluations and supplier risk management. Based on the strategic potential and the performance of the supplier, different interaction models are defined. According to the most recent Kearney global Assessment of Excellence in Procurement survey, companies following this logic have a much better performance and return on their SRM than those who do not. Using digital tools, supplier segmentation can be automated, as well as supplier interaction. Automated interactions may include onboarding, providing information or risk monitoring.
  - *Operating Process Management:* Those companies that have developed efficient and lean processes have a head start creating a powerful procurement function. A well-defined process can more easily be transferred to RPA, and it's simple to introduce process tracking. This allows companies to focus on the right things and avoid firefighting.
- *Supporting Processes (the foundation of the House):*
  - *Performance Management:* With digital tools, companies can more easily define metrics and targets and track their progress toward their goals. These

3

Digital and advanced analytics enabled

Supply
Management
Strategy

Organizational Alignment

Sourcing &
category
management

Supplier
relationship
management

Operating
process
management

Performance
management

Information,
analytics and
knowledge
management

Talent management

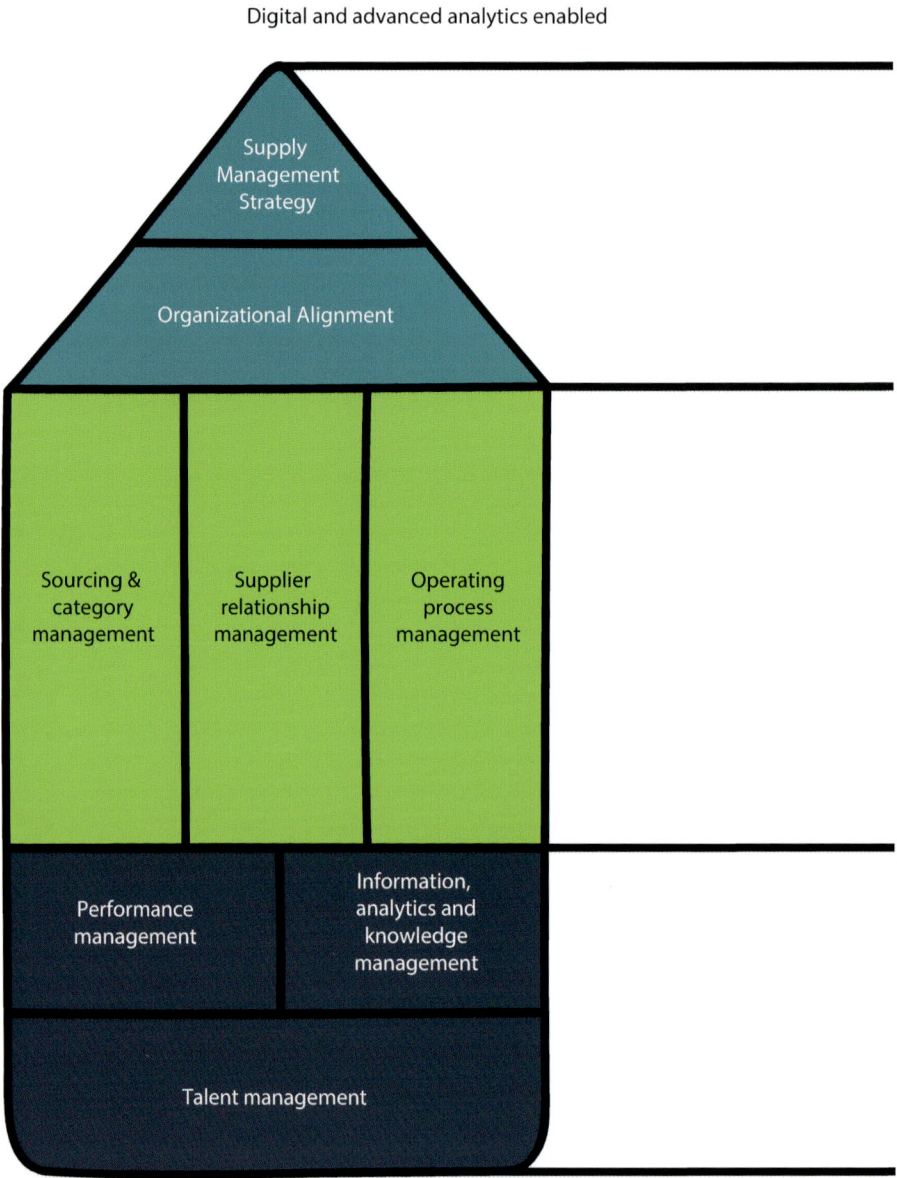

KEARNEY HOUSE OF PURCHASING & SUPPLY ^{SM}

◘ Fig. 3.1 House of Purchasing and Supply with technologies and tools for efficiency and effectiveness

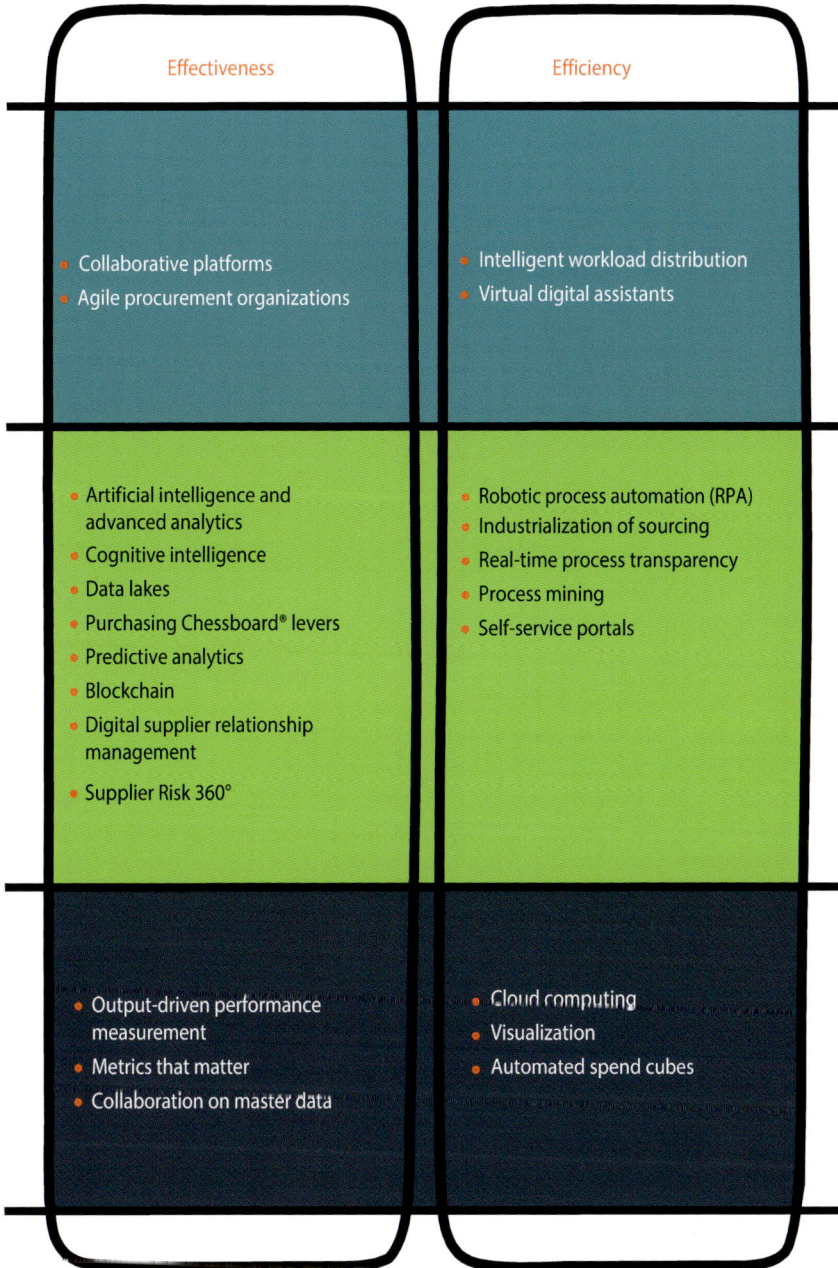

Effectiveness	Efficiency
• Collaborative platforms • Agile procurement organizations	• Intelligent workload distribution • Virtual digital assistants
• Artificial intelligence and advanced analytics • Cognitive intelligence • Data lakes • Purchasing Chessboard® levers • Predictive analytics • Blockchain • Digital supplier relationship management • Supplier Risk 360°	• Robotic process automation (RPA) • Industrialization of sourcing • Real-time process transparency • Process mining • Self-service portals
• Output-driven performance measurement • Metrics that matter • Collaboration on master data	• Cloud computing • Visualization • Automated spend cubes

3

indicators can also make reporting faster and more informative. One of the most important metrics to watch in procurement is ROSMA, or Return on Supply Management Assets, which compares procurement costs, like personnel, to the savings it delivers. The visualization of the metrics can help procurement communicate its successes more effectively.

- *Information, Analytics and Knowledge Management:* "If we only knew what we actually know!" many procurement executives bemoan. In most cases, companies do have access to more information than what they are using, for instance information about suppliers and categories that is received from web or news crawlers. Having information well organized and ready to use creates a competitive advantage. In a study on digital procurement conducted by Kearney in early 2019, we found that 92 percent of procurement professionals store information about RFPs that have closed, as well as RFP templates, in a structured way in knowledge management tools. This compares with just 33 percent who keep information about supplier collaboration, best practices and sourcing strategies in a structured way in knowledge management tools.
- *HR Management:* Attracting the best people outside and inside the organization for procurement jobs is an important differentiator of powerful procurement organizations. This calls for a change of working style and focus because top talent wants to do interesting, non-repetitive work that makes an impact. Many such employees are interested in agile working methods and client-centric roles. Separately, some OEMs have achieved procurement excellence, which makes it easier for them to attract high-potential talent, while other companies have even made procurement a board-level function, thereby increasing its attractiveness.

As mentioned, Kearney summarized these dimensions in its House of Purchasing and Supply in the early 1990s. With the advent of digital, the dimensions remain the same, but the way of working will change completely in all dimensions. The function will be much more powerful, much more connected and much faster than before, with the ability to focus on the value add, not on the administration of tasks.

How have digital tools and advanced analytics impacted the different dimensions of the House in terms of efficiency and effectiveness?

On the following pages, we examine just this.

Level 1: Procurement Strategy & Organization – Effectiveness

Procurement organizations need to be more dynamic and agile because of digitalization, and it is digital tools and technologies that will help procurement change and improve. Because of this, we expect significant changes to the procurement organization. We expect to see much smaller departments that will focus mostly on strategic tasks – while tactical and operational procurement processes are either outsourced or automated. Personnel costs are not likely to decrease even if headcount does, because companies will need to pay more for strategists and experts focused on analytics and agile working methods.

Finally, we anticipate that procurement will become less focused on categories and more focused on projects that include category experts and project managers skilled in using digital tools.

Here we examine technologies, tools and organizational changes that can boost the effectiveness of procurement strategy and organization.

Collaborative Platforms

Digitalization helps companies communicate more closely internally and with external suppliers. In general, there are two types of collaborative platforms that can improve the effectiveness of procurement:

- *Internal collaborative platforms:* Innovation in business communication often evolves from private life. Think of chat groups, cloud-based file sharing and asynchronous messaging (such as WhatsApp). Similar online social tools are now available to procurement professionals, and their use can lead to significantly higher productivity. Some examples are idea-generation platforms shared between procurement and R&D and interaction forums for employees and senior management.

   The platforms may also offer features for internal communication, task distribution, file sharing and deadline monitoring. Software providers such as Signavio or Celonis offer such tools. Many also support remote work, giving employees more flexibility for parental leave, for example. These tools enable people to work more efficiently through better and more communication, and they can be used to collect the materials needed to solve certain problems or finish certain tasks. All in all, this boosts effectiveness.

- *External collaborative platforms:* External collaborative platforms shared with suppliers can make a big difference in the innovation process. They can help employees keep an innovation mindset for the long-term, not just for specific projects. Such platforms make it easy to communicate about ways to improve processes, new technologies and new production techniques.

   All of these ideas can derive from closer and more frequent interaction and collaboration between suppliers and customers. To make procurement part of the innovation process on an everyday basis, procurement professionals must be able to work across different functions.

   They must also process new ideas from suppliers, for example by using innovation management software for continuously reviewing and scoring new ideas until they are approved. Using such tools can help procurement more actively search for and support innovation and work more closely with R&D and senior management at the supplier.

Another important area where external collaborative platforms can improve processes are with tenders and negotiations with suppliers. Some tools help buyers select the right game-theory based negotiation strategies. Others, like Coupa (formerly Trade Extensions), make it easier to onboard suppliers, give them information automatically, and see if information is outstanding from submitted quotes,

3

purchase orders or invoices. Tools also exist for programmatic media buying or target costing with statistical support (StatTools).

With these type of digital tools, the location and number of suppliers becomes less important. For instance, with the Coupa tender functionality, users can run parallel, game-theory based negotiations and get multiple hundreds and millions of price quotes. Such tools will have a high impact on categories with highly standardized specifications. They have been used successfully in many categories, such as in indirects, like packaging and logistics.

These bidding tools can help users analyze millions of quotes, replacing spreadsheet-based analytics tools that are still in use in many procurement organizations. They also support procurement in buying globally, if that is the stated goal, because the platforms allow suppliers from remote or rural areas to participate. With the help of translation capabilities, like Google Translate, all users can communicate, regardless of their language.

Agile Procurement Organizations

An agile organizational setup in procurement means that select teams work with the agile methodology. These teams do a large part of the tasks typically performed by the category management team but do so with techniques such as huddles, scrums and sprints. The teams are set up this way to keep procurement from focusing too narrowly on categories. The teams help procurement increase process efficiency, cut back on downtime between tenders and engage better with suppliers.

Typically, the teams are staffed cross-functionally to ensure diverse thinking but also to make sure cross-functional objectives and decision-making power is properly represented. Teams may have specific objectives such as doing "should-cost" calculations, designing the negotiation strategies using game theory, or getting a particular sourcing job done faster. Frequently, teams are set up for a short period of time or for specific events. With an organization that supports an agile approach, companies can replace suppliers with new ones faster, which can lead to cost savings.

Often, teams working in this manner have specific competencies related to the objective but do not have specific category know-how. Therefore, in modern procurement organizations, these teams will move from category to category to challenge the status-quo and find ways to deliver new value.

Agile teams must work fast and flexibly and need powerful digital tools at hand, such as project management tools and category or process-specific tools. The tools must be accessible to all team members and include real-time information to enable fully automated cross-functional interactions. In addition, working with such teams requires a leadership style that rewards people for taking their own initiatives, accepts failure and congratulates success.

Level 1: Procurement Strategy & Organization – Efficiency

Now let's look at tools and technologies that influence efficiency in procurement supply and organization.

Intelligent Workload Distribution

Intelligent workload distribution tools dynamically distribute work across a group of people, giving individuals those tasks that they are best-suited to handle. To run as intended, systems must incorporate an in-depth understanding of the business context. For instance, if the service procurement provides to its internal customers is of utmost importance, the system must be programmed to reflect this. The system captures which tasks need to be done, assigns a value to those tasks and distributes them. Such tools can help managers assign and reassign tasks directly from an app when they conduct the morning meeting. Intelligent workload distribution tools can improve the efficiency and effectiveness of customer service and keep people flexible about what they are working on, since priorities and tasks can be shifted quickly within the system.

Virtual Digital Assistants

Virtual digital assistants are AI-enabled chatbots which can communicate with procurement professionals, for instance by taking verbal instruction to search for orders and purchase requests using vendor and item names. Another example is a bot initiating a conversation with a buyer about an event, such as bad weather in a particular location, and making suggestions about the options that a buyer has in the aftermath of the event (such as buy the commodity elsewhere). Procurement professionals speak to the bot to instruct it.

Level 2: Core Processes – Effectiveness

With digital tools and technologies, core processes in procurement can become more effective because companies have new ways to impact business outcomes. Here you'll find more about a wide variety of tools and technologies and how they are making core procurement processes more effective.

Artificial Intelligence (AI)

AI is a collection of machine-learning technologies that can improve the effectiveness of many dimensions of the House of Purchasing and Supply by enabling humans and machines to make better decisions and executing on those decisions. It includes natural language processing, computer visioning, pattern recognition, and reasoning and optimization capabilities as examples. In procurement, AI can be found in chatbots that recognize the voice of a buyer who is requesting the status of an invoice. Or procurement can make better predictions of demand with pattern recognition analyses of large data sets.

Another example is reasoning and optimization capabilities that enable computers to deduce. The important point here is that in parts of the organization, humans will no longer be needed due to AI, computers and robots taking over some of the low value-adding tasks.

Applications of AI in procurement may include the following.

- *Natural language processing (NLP)*, which includes speech recognition, natural language understanding and natural language generation. Typical use cases are:

- Asking bots for invoices and status updates, where the bot checks the status on an internal system and responds. Similar to Amazon's Alexa.
- Purchasing of goods. Asking a bot to issue a purchase order to the vendor or provide a recommendation for suppliers. The bot understands the requests and searches databases for answers.
- Negotiation. Trained bots can negotiate. Their tactics get better and better, the more training they have. They can negotiate via email or voice and work similarly to bots in call centers.
- *Computer visioning* means the recognition of texts and graphics by computers.
  - A potential use case is for invoices and PO's. They can be scanned and their content is recognized by optical character recognition (OCR) technology. This saves time on filling out forms and data fields.
- *Pattern recognition applications may include:*
  - *Spend pattern recognition.* Based on a training set of data, algorithms can cluster and clean supplier data and classifications, perhaps more accurately than a human.
  - *Predictions*, for instance predictions about the effect of commodity price changes on end product prices.
- *Reasoning and optimization are the ability of computers to make logical deductions.*
  - In procurement, this can help with *supplier risk identification.* Algorithms can analyze news and (social) media feeds to form meaningful conclusions or create word clouds for evaluating suppliers.

As AI becomes more widespread and even more powerful, we expect further procurement applications, such as OCR for recognizing not only structured data but also unstructured data, and NLP for recognizing spoken languages, regardless of accents.

Advanced Analytics

Until now, procurement departments typically generated a lot of data but did not realize the full potential of using this data via analytics. We have seen that procurement organizations using advanced analytics typically increase their savings considerably. Advanced analytics use algorithms to recognize patterns in complex data sets, and it allows procurement analysts to query all their data, determine the statistically significant drivers of analyses, and cluster the data according to those drivers.

When comparing the differentiating factors of leaders and followers, we see already today that 90 percent of leaders use predictive analytics, AI-enabled analytics (e.g., parametric bidding, collaborative optimization) or anticipatory analytics (e.g., should-cost, TCO, scenario modeling). This compares to only 18 percent for followers. In fact, some 42 percent of followers were using spreadsheet tools and traditional analytics (e.g., for bid comparison), according to the AEP.

In general, the progression steps for using advanced analytics are *descriptive* ("How did my category spend develop over the last three years?"), *diagnostic* ("Why did my category spend increase over the last three months?"), *predictive* ("How are prices expected to develop for a particular commodity?") and *prescriptive* ("Should we build a new warehouse?").

In procurement, analytics may be applied in different ways:

- *Supplier-related analysis:* Making better decisions on suppliers for strategic product categories, assessing new suppliers for existing product categories, monitoring supplier-attrition risk, providing insight for fraud-detection, and making predictions among suppliers.
- *Category analysis:* Understanding suppliers' raw-material requirements and facilitating what-if scenario analysis, such as estimates of the potential costs of changing suppliers.
- *Contract analysis:* Optimizing supplier compliance — for example cost, lead time and number of contracts. Also, improving contract management — for example, optimization of contract duration for single source vs. multi-source contracts.
- *Payment analysis:* Optimizing supplier payments and credit periods.
- *Process-related analysis:* Mining processes to identify maverick actions.

Along with implementing these capabilities, companies need to ensure that staff with the right skills is handling the analyses, and training should be offered on how to include the outcome of various analyses into negotiations.

Cognitive Intelligence

Cognitive intelligence is the individual technologies that perform specific tasks that facilitate human intelligence. It involves analyzing data, identifying patterns, including those that are not visible to humans, and accumulating know-how. The results of the analyses are presented to human employees so they can make a decision on a specific matter.

Used in procurement, cognitive intelligence systems can generate information that can help human buyers make a decision, such as reports from internal transaction data and business rules, and/or external market data. Reports can present new ideas for further action by a category manager.

Examples include a company that needed to have a real-time overview of the impact of particular commodity prices on its production. It implemented an interactive commodity tracking platform linked to procurement strategy, which provided those details. The system gave a clear recommendation on what to do, and the buyer could accept or reject it.

The next development step would be a comparison of what the system recommended vs. what the buyer actually did, and how the market evolved in the meantime. Such analyses and transparency will help users gain confidence in the accuracy of recommendations generated by cognitive intelligence systems.

Data Lakes

Internal data from enterprise resource planning (ERP) systems, business data warehouses and other sources are regularly used for analyses conducted by the procurement organization; now, with large external data sets also being used, those analyses are becoming broader and richer. These sources of data are combined in data lakes via technologies like Apache Hadoop and are then accessible via the cloud or on-premise solutions. They can be used for procurement analyses based on AI and/or accessed via a unified interface. Due to data lakes, procurement can do far more sophisticated analyses than in the past, and data is accessible faster, since it is already consolidated.

3

Data lakes, which are repositories of data usually kept in the original format, are usually built with four different types of data:

- Internal structured data, such as data from ERP and data warehouse systems, as well as master or transactional data
- Internal unstructured data. This data can be from technical drawings or text-based information, such as quality assessments. It can also come from internal audio or video files.
- External structured data. This data comes from data providers and usually contains market or supplier information, as well as other data, such as weather data.
- External unstructured data. An example of this type of data is data from social media, forums or web pages that can be scraped. Audio and video data fit here, too.

A data lake was the basis of a tool implemented by a German automotive company with suppliers in Asia. It needed to anticipate extreme weather events to safeguard its production and supply chain. The automotive company used a social media monitoring tool to get early warnings of potential earthquakes based on the chatter and queries of people in a certain region. The company is now working on implementing these early warnings into production and logistic decisions.

Purchasing Chessboard® Levers

Kearney developed the Purchasing Chessboard® to structure procurement strategies across industries. Levers are defined by category according to the balance between the supply power of the supplier and the demand power of the customer. The Purchasing Chessboard's® 64 squares provide users with methods that can be applied individually, or in combination, to reduce costs and improve relationships with suppliers. Many methods on the Purchasing Chessboard® can be used in procurement far more often than they already are to help buyers find new and different ways to work.[1]

Although the basic principles of supply and demand are not changing due to digitalization, digitalization is having a big impact on category sourcing strategies. Advanced analytics makes it possible to improve procurement strategies, and digital procurement tools are becoming interactive knowledge toolkits.

Digitalization will improve how Purchasing Chessboard® strategies can be implemented, and it may change those strategies altogether. For example, a supplier fitness program working with advanced digital tools will be able to plan deliverables more quickly or optimize routes so that the supplier can deliver services for less. In some cases, entirely new strategies can be introduced, such as those supported by new analytical models or new partnership models. An example is Amazon's B2B offering, which is changing how companies think about C-spend. It brings together a platform with a very easy to handle ordering system.

---

1   Please find out more at: ▶ https://www.kearney.com/web/the-purchasing-chessboard

Predictive Analytics

In many categories, procurement teams face frequent commodity price volatility, for instance for raw materials needed for production. Now, companies can make better pricing forecasts with digital tools that analyze historical data and monitor ongoing risks, for instance by monitoring news and social media.

Kearney has developed such a tool which allows users to generate pricing estimates – for example for cocoa beans – for two to three months in advance and adjust their hedging and procurement strategies accordingly. The algorithm gets trained on the data set and adjusts parameters based on what it "learns" from each analysis. Users can receive an alert when commodity prices change with suggestions for resulting price effects.

Predictive analytics are also improving demand forecasts, sometimes called demand sensing. Ideally, predictive analytics is built into a tool which can identify correlations between internal demand data and external data.

Blockchain

Blockchain is a new technology that has the potential to disrupt B2B transactions to the same degree that the internet disrupted communications. Blockchain is a list of records, called blocks, which are linked to one another using cryptography. When a transaction is made – and the parties agree to its details – the transaction is encoded into a block of digital data and uniquely signed. As further transactions are made, the blocks are "chained" together, creating the so-called blockchain.

Currently, business transactions such as orders, payments and shipments are tracked in the individual records of each participant in a transaction. This can lead to differing versions that lead to further error, fraud and inefficiency. When parties use a single, shared, tamper-evident ledger, however, all participants can share a common end-to-end view of all the transactions.

Blockchain has potential in procurement, since blockchain could make the source-to-pay process significantly more efficient, provide transparency about transactions and build trust about the transaction data.

Specifically, blockchain has application in:

- Spend data: Spend data can be stored on a blockchain-based distributed ledger to provide improved transparency along the value chain. In combination with advanced analytics, large volumes of transparent spend data can be used to generate a vast number of insights that will make doing business more predictable for a broad ecosystem of partners.
- Contracting: Blockchain can be the basis for programs that provide tamper-proof contracts that automatically implement contractual terms or payments when certain conditions are met. Blockchain could also help implement complex multi-party contracts along the value chain.
- Order management: Procurement can use blockchain-based solutions to validate and approve orders without intermediaries, to process invoices and to match the invoice to the PO. Critical supplier credentials, certificates and qualification statuses can be stored on a blockchain so they cannot be forged or compromised.

- Supply chain transparency and traceability: Blockchain can ensure authenticity and traceability of all goods throughout the purchasing cycle. Verifiable trails of suppliers' goods will be established. It will be much easier to review supplier credentials and reduce fraud.

3

As an aside, if blockchain-based cryptocurrencies become accepted tender, procurement will need to increase its knowledge about how to handle the currency.

Digital Supplier Relationship Management

In many organizations, Supplier Relationship Management (SRM) is actually a form of "Supplier Performance Management" in which strategic potential is not really measured. Companies use transaction-oriented KPIs and cross-functional feedback to put pressure on suppliers to perform better, instead of using digital SRM for innovation management and to help suppliers improve in a structured and continuous way. Today, one of the most important assets of any firm is its ecosystem of partners, and properly managing such ecosystems is critical. Procurement is already accustomed to managing large and complex ecosystems, but as this process becomes more digital, SRM will change:

- First, *a single well-structured and formal SRM program* needs to be implemented within the organization. This program needs to manage ecosystem partners along the entire value chain. The most critical capability of the program is to distinguish in which areas the company requires strategic partnership, for instance by using a make vs. buy analysis or alignment with the strategy departments. The single SRM program must also be used to distinguish the right partners for the requirements and define how to operationalize the relationship with those partners. Having these distinctions among suppliers will help buyers as they shift their focus to strategic partners and let automated systems and bots "manage" relationships with the non-strategic suppliers. This focus will also enable buyers to become more deeply integrated with their strategic partners and get the most from the relationship.
- Second, *supplier performance feedback will become more relevant, comprehensive and transparent,* as more processes become digital. Analytics of the data generated with SRM systems will enable procurement to more easily monitor trends and priorities in the relationship. Procurement should be able to retrieve everything related to the relationship that is within the organization, including email history, meeting recordings, project history and video feedback. This will enable 360° "health checks" of the relationship. We also expect rating systems that have matured in the B2C space, such as those used on eBay or Amazon, to be used more often in B2B interactions, as it can be seen on portals such as Alibaba. The ratings will include anonymized risk scores from external rating agencies, as well as the feedback a supplier got from other customers. This level of detail will help companies make faster decisions about new suppliers. Furthermore, by comparing a suppliers' performance at your own company with its reviews by other customers, companies can better understand if the root cause of problems lies with the supplier or with your own organization. Finally, we expect buying firms to more actively seek feedback from suppliers

to improve continuously. At Kearney, we regularly ask suppliers about their experience in different areas to assess collaboration and get ideas for process improvements.

- Third, organizations should make *supplier innovation an integral part of their own innovation strategy.* Already today, external innovations account for a significant part of buying firms' overall innovations. We predict that across industries, this will increase to well above 50 percent by 2025. In addition, in industrialized countries, we expect the percentage of employees working outside of formal employment structures to increase to above 50 percent. Companies need a defined and focused open-innovation strategy to make use of supplier knowledge and capabilities in support of overall business innovation and growth. Companies should track supplier contributions to innovation using select metrics. Big data and AI will make it easier for companies to find those suppliers who are strong at innovation because of vastly improved abilities to identify those companies and conduct custom analyses. Already today, startups such as scoutbee and Supplier.ai use AI-based tools to find innovative solutions to business challenges.
- Fourth, expect firms to use a variety of ways to *track and anticipate supplier-related risks.* These may include audits, KPI monitoring, scenario and contingency planning, predictive modeling and simulation. The scope of the supplier–related risks to monitor may include financial, environmental, health and safety, and intellectual property protection risks, as well as those related to reputation and business continuity. Procurement will also continuously monitor risks along the extended supply chain and will have rapid response/recovery protocols in place to manage risk events when they occur. Digital supply chain orchestration platforms will allow companies to monitor indicators comprehensively and in real time. One example is the platform provided by Elementum.
- Fifth, *we expect data sharing and transparency to transform relationships.* The sharing of data in real-time, such as forecasts and capacity restrictions, will bring buyers and suppliers into closer cooperation within a growing ecosystem. Digital and connected supply chains will be based on real-time data and shared databases, and they will be oriented to the end customer. Supplier management will mean having preventive, standardized and sustainable control of supplier networks with end-to-end visibility of supply, costs, margins and performance.

With the increasing availability of supplier price and performance data, suppliers will be ever more replaceable, which will further increase the pressure on suppliers to differentiate.

Also, crowdsourcing for products, services and ideas will become more common. In crowdsourcing, purchasing experts typically go into an active dialog with suppliers during the prototyping phase and explain the product specifications they want. This gives a company the advantage of not carrying all the costs of development and pre-production but still being able to tailor crowd-sourced products to their preferences.

Finally, we expect SRM activities currently focused on Tier-1 suppliers to extend to suppliers further down the value chain, since digital tools enable communication and additional supplier transparency, for instance via supplier collaboration

3

platforms. Companies such as Whole Foods and Starbucks, as well as most in the automotive industry, are paving the way in this area by creating partnerships and conducting SRM activities with Tier-2 and Tier-3 suppliers.

These points will require organizations to invest significant resources in identifying the best external partners, attracting the most innovative supply partners to do business with the buying firm, contracting these partners, integrating their innovations and ensuring they provide their product or service only to the buying firm. If firms are able to integrate these activities into their SRM processes, they will be able to achieve significant innovations in products, processes, services and business models.

Supply Risk 360°

Supply Risk 360° is a new way of looking at a supply chain by assessing how different types of external events influence it. In the past, companies had to wait until their suppliers told them that a part of the supply chain was experiencing problems because of a pre-supplier; now buyers can have visibility into the full supply chain via tools that show the locations of pre-producers and send alerts if external events could endanger delivery. The benefit is the early warning system, which enables the buyer to react, inform production or look for a substitute.

External events can be more easily identifiable events like extreme weather conditions and natural disasters, but also financial crises, regionally or within a single company, and changes in the social fabric, such as strikes, civil unrest or epidemics.

The systemic risk screening does not only identify the crisis and the geolocation but also the affected area and any infrastructure that exists for companies in these areas. A scoring model with more than 80 different criteria then assigns a score to this event that indicates severity.

The system is then able to derive the impact of the event on the market by modeling the changes in available supply within the affected region and how the markets will react when demand shifts to other regions. At the same time, an alert can be triggered, informing the category manager so that the risk can be assessed and appropriate actions taken. These alerts can be made very specific by modeling the supply chain of the company. If a modeled supply chain is impacted, the system will know precisely which parts are impacted and what the effect is going to be, both in the market and in terms of availability of raw materials or intermediate products.

Level 2: Core Processes – Efficiency

Digital tools and solutions can make sourcing and managing procurement processes faster and cheaper, and fewer people are needed to accomplish the same things. Below find more on specific tools and technologies and their applications to procurement.

Robotic Process Automation

Robotic process automation (RPA) is changing the way organizations complete tasks and helping them become significantly more efficient. RPA is a software automation tool for rules-based tasks that automates simple, existing, and routine processes and performs them faster, cheaper, and with less errors than humans can do them. Frequently, RPA scripts are embedded into a "smart workflow" which integrates tasks performed by groups of humans and machines. This enables the end-to-end tracking of processes in real time. RPA has demonstrated the following benefits:

- *Accuracy*: Consistent execution of processes and elimination of data inconsistency
- *Speed*: More than 20 times faster than humans and a significant reduction in cycle time
- *Transparency*: Easy tracking and reporting of errors and root causes
- *Scalability*: Scalable on demand and across unrelated processes
- *Value*: Typically, with a positive ROI within the first year

RPA represents a significant opportunity for modern procurement organizations, since more than 50 percent of operational tasks in procurement are repetitive. The areas in procurement which would benefit most from RPA are:

- *Spend data*: Bots can be used to maintain spend and vendor data.
- *Contracting*: Bots could review contracts and compare them against standard terms and conditions.
- *Sourcing*: More advanced bots can be used to compare current pricing and support the execution of RFI and RFP processes. In addition, bots can be used to ensure compliance to preferred suppliers and to contracts.
- *Supplier relationship management*: Bots can keep certain criteria about supplier segmentation up to date by automatically gathering and evaluating quantitative and qualitative performance metrics based on rules.
- *Risk management*: Bots can conduct supplier due diligence across several risk categories by gathering data and comparing it to KPIs.
- *Payments*: Bots are already being used to validate supplier invoices and to initiate payments.

Industrialization of Sourcing

The industrialization of sourcing is the holistic automation of the sourcing process via various tools and bots, and the integration of bots and human interaction (see ◘ Fig. 3.2). These bots make the whole process more effective and efficient, and implementing them requires a detailed knowledge of the tool landscape and processes.

For some companies, tendering bots are still something completely new. Imagine a requisitioner from R&D needs equipment for testing or for a product teardown – for example something that has not been sourced before. This person must first enter a requisition into the system in a structured way. Then a bot takes over the request and does what a procurement professional would have done before: screen the supply market. The bot is looking for different offerings from different suppliers by scanning the market and its suppliers.

Alternatively, the bot can look at the internal supplier list and select the suppliers with the best rating and analyze supplier reviews.

In the next step, the bot returns with a proposal and/ or a recommendation about things such as which supplier to choose, shipping, product availability, etc. From a systems perspective, the bot could then go ahead and place the order.

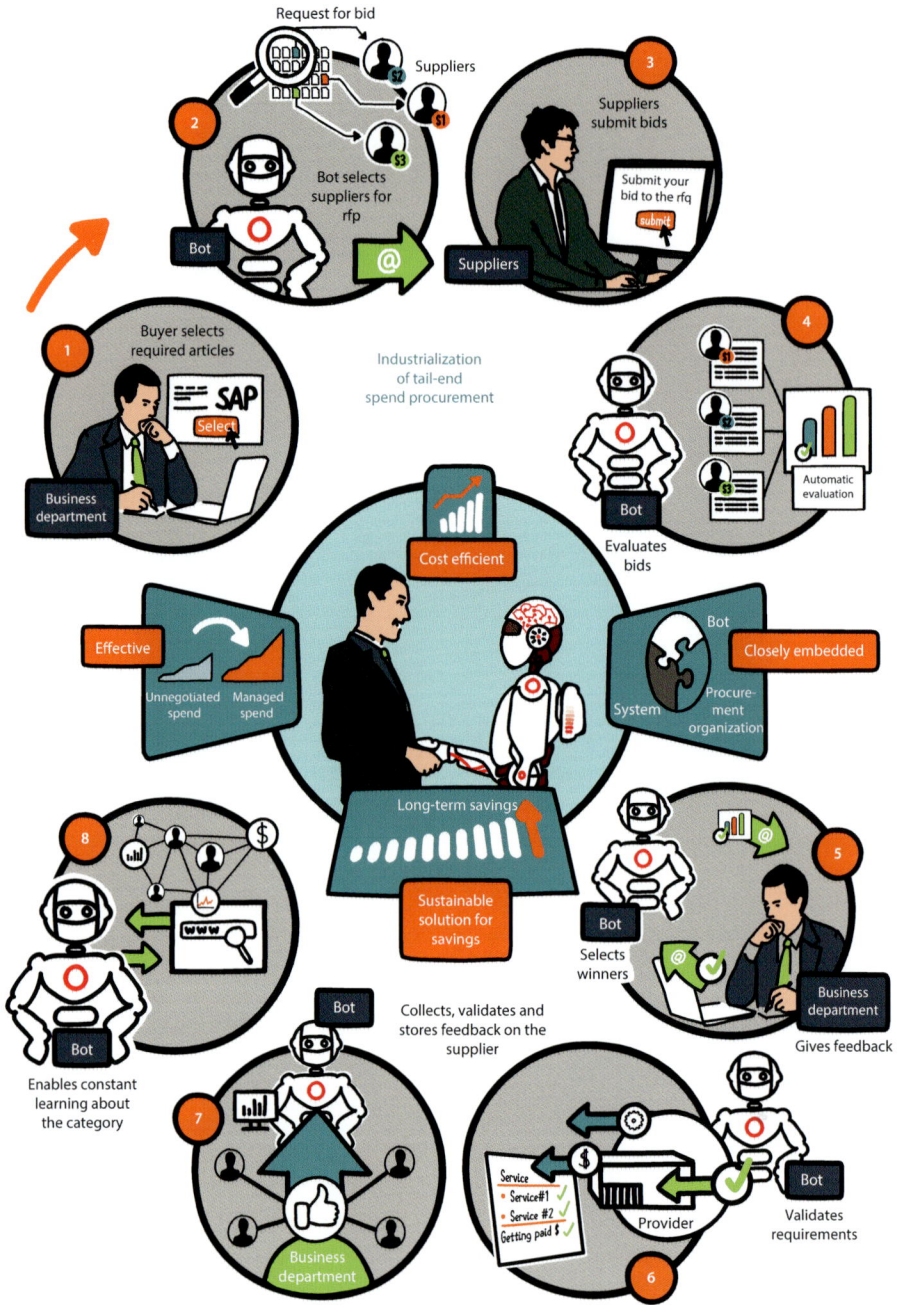

Fig. 3.2   Steps to automated tail-end spend with bots

When Kearney implemented a similar bot-based process for a client, the system was designed so that a human user could make the final decision on which product to buy, and the bot would then proceed with the order. Once the decision was made, the bot takes over all the paperwork that would have had to be done in a manual system, like creating a purchase order. Upon delivery, the invoice can be paid automatically.

This approach is particularly good for indirect, tail-end spend, since it still has limitations when the products are unique or not structured. Still, the areas of application are growing.

Real-Time Process Transparency with Consolidated, Clean Data

In most companies, data is still collected by division and often in separate IT systems. Each division may have a different means of collecting data and collect widely diverse data. Sometimes this means that multiple divisions in a company have conflicting views on a matter because they have each analyzed different data.

To reach a point of real-time process transparency, data must be merged and harmonized across the enterprise. Only then is it possible to connect dots and derive insights that can improve process efficiency. The effort is Herculean and is a common reason that companies do not use advanced analytics to their full potential. But going through the effort of harmonizing data helps more than just procurement; it is also critical for supply chain management and optimization, production, R&D and more. When companies have put their data in order, they can better visualize their processes, understand their own strengths and weaknesses, and steer processes more effectively to decrease lead times. They are then ready for the next step on the maturity ladder: AI-enabled process monitoring and steering to automatically re-engineer processes as needed.

Process Mining

Process mining is used to analyze the steps someone takes to complete a task. By continuing to gather this data over time, the system can start to see where bottlenecks occur or where inefficiencies lie within the process. The system can also give feedback about non-compliance with process steps. Process mining tools can be used to calculate how long process steps take, compare this to the planned time and then assess why differences occur. In procurement, process mining is often used to analyze maverick buying and make suggestions about how it can be avoided. An example of a process mining tool is Celonis.

Self-Service Portals

Self-service portals improve efficiency, since they help users work more independently. In procurement, they can help in the following areas:

- *Purchasing C-articles.* C-articles typically make up 5 percent of a company's spend but 80 percent of the sourcing transactions. In the past, employees had several platforms for purchasing items that were small and needed to be bought in bulk. One was for typical office supplies, and another for maintenance, repair and operations services, as an example. In the worst case, companies used no portal at all and employees bought small items from the corner store. With

3

the integration of B2B portals, such as Amazon Business, buying C-articles becomes easier because of the wide variety of products on offer, the ability to purchase in a company-compliant way, and POs and invoices sent directly to the company. These portals also make it easy for users to track orders and manage invoices.

— *Automated supplier registration.* Other portals, like supplier portals at companies, let procurement professionals benefit from automated supplier registration. That registration generates master data that can be managed on the portal, including a change of contact person at a supplier, an updated address, or changes to supplier certificates.

Level 3: Supporting Processes – Effectiveness

In supporting processes, companies can focus on defining targets and tracking them with digital tools to become more effective. This is important because of the new ways buyers are working. For instance, many are given incentives, such as financial incentives or points in an appraisal, to reduce the cycle time of procuring a certain item. In addition, buyers must adapt to faster reporting cycles with their reporting on project outcomes, like savings achieved. Here we discuss tools and technologies to help support processes in procurement become more effective.

Output-Driven Performance Measurement

As procurement becomes more strategic, its KPIs need to change. Performance should be a measure of outputs or outcomes, not of the amount of work or number of tenders conducted.

Kearney developed a performance management system for a confectionary client in Europe to measure the impact of procurement on commodity categories. The company had a system in place to track how different factors impacted price and demand, as well as to monitor foreign currency rates and negotiations with suppliers, but it did not combine this with an analysis of how prices changed. At the same time, procurement professionals in each category followed a different approach. The system we developed:

— Separated savings targets that were already planned during budget revisions and those savings that occurred sporadically during the year, due to dips in commodity prices

— Incorporated external market information about commodity trading prices to analyze historical prices and create forecasts of price trends. Procurement could then show the prices it achieved for different categories, compared to average market prices.

— Created standard contracting models for each category, such as a method to consistently buy commodities at fixed prices for a fixed period over a year. Such models make it possible to see the positive or negative impact on achieved commodity prices resulting from decisions by category managers that were not made using the model.

Metrics that Matter

When talking about performance management and KPIs, begin with three points made by William Edwards Deming:

- You cannot manage what you cannot measure
- You cannot measure what you cannot define
- You cannot define what you cannot understand

To set up an effective KPI framework, companies must thoroughly understand how their business goals can be expressed quantitatively, for example with the right KPIs linked to the right data sources. Those KPIs should lead to actionable insights for managing the business.

Performance management is not a new discipline, but many companies still do not track all indicators that are important and follow through on insights consistently.

Often, analyses are based solely on internal data; however, if external data is used as well, such as that available on markets, consumers, weather, and via social media, companies can produce metrics that are far more insightful. As a result, they would be able to better drill down on the root causes of weak performance.

Of course, metrics must be presented in a way that they do not overwhelm analysts and decision makers, for instance via dashboards that allow users to view standard, template reports and create custom ones.

Collaboration on Master Data

The poor state of master data in many companies is the root cause of many problems, including incomplete or even misleading analyses. Typically, companies try to clean up the master data themselves or hire external support to do a master data cleanup exercise. Companies can also release cleansed and verified data records to a blockchain and then use that blockchain, full of information supplied by others, to validate even more of their master data. This can be an effective way to cleanse master data across group subsidiaries as well.

Level 3: Supporting Processes – Efficiency

Supporting processes need to be fast and easy to administer to give procurement professionals more time to work on higher-level tasks, such as structuring spend cubes and understanding analyses. Here are technologies and tools that are helping.

Cloud Computing

Cloud computing is computing via remote servers and computer resources that can be quickly provided at costs that are lower than it would be to keep these resources locally. Some advantages are the flexibility of cloud services and the quick availability of increased computing capacity. As cloud computing has caught on, it has enabled business models and platform sharing because the cloud makes it easy to share data, for instance among all involved in a supply chain. Cloud computing has the potential to drastically change the way SRM is done because it allows real-time sharing of information among all parties in a supply chain. Cloud computing has also brought quicker access to solutions that speed up operational procurement processes. And it makes the joint development of products and services with suppliers easier, for instance on a platform.

3

Visualization

When information is made visual, people can understand it more quickly and begin to work with it faster. Because there is so much data in procurement and it is so complex, data visualization is particularly important. Procurement professionals have come to expect dashboard-style compilations of the results of their analyses served up in a visually-appealing manner. These dashboards will provide procurement with a real-time overview of category spend and history, for example. They can also be used for creating forecasts. Visualizations are not just for buyers, though. They are becoming more commonplace for people at all levels of an organization.

Automated Spend Cubes

Spend cubes are clusters of data about how much was spent, with whom it was spent and when it was spent, for example. Category strategies begin with the collection and compilation of purchase order and invoice data as well as the codification of that data. As a basis for further digitalization, companies need full reports for each cube that are updated automatically and made visual for quick understanding.

Usually, companies struggle with wrongly coded supplier names, spend data that is in different currencies, or data that is unclear or wrong because the manual entry was wrong. Applications that are based on AI can make spend categorization faster and more precise. In such applications, the spend processing algorithm gets "smarter" – for example, it works more accurately after being trained on large amounts of data. Ideally, companies would have their new POs and invoices automatically allocated to a spend cube, which the CPO can easily analyze in a visual manner at the desktop or on a mobile device.

Most companies are able to aggregate their spend cube data and cleanse it sufficiently with digital tools, but they will probably still need humans to make sure that the data is categorized correctly.

Automated spend cubes are the basis for a variety of important analyses, including price spreads on articles and demand forecasts. Typically, data in automated spend cubes comes from data lakes, where data of different structures and from different sources is combined. That data is then mined, converted (if necessary), and analyzed. Metrics are designed and the results of analyses are made visual. All this feeds into other digital tools, such as those for market sensing, predictive analytics and output-driven performance management.

Achieving spend transparency should be a top priority for every procurement department because spend data is the basis for so many decisions and is of keen interest to the company's top managers.

73 **3**

What Are Procurement Leaders Doing Differently than Others in Digital?

What Are Procurement Leaders Doing Differently than Others in Digital?

Based on our continuous Assessment of Excellence in Procurement survey, which has been conducted every two to three years since 1992 and includes accumulated data from more than 10,000 participants, Kearney has determined the procurement topics that are on executives' minds. The latest study shows that those companies in the leading cohort for procurement use a wider range of digital tools and technologies, and/or use them more frequently, than those companies that are not in the leading cohort. Both leaders and laggards frequently use digital tools for ERP, but in relatively new areas, such as cloud computing, advanced data visualizations, social media analyses, and collaboration platforms, leaders have a higher adoption.

We also observed that leading procurement departments are focused on hiring people with data analytics skills that are equivalent to what is needed to work as a strategic buyer. Leaders in procurement have already increased their efficiency with further automation and are now turning their attention to how to use data to increase effectiveness.

Procurement departments must secure funding for their own digital roadmaps by helping top management understand the ways in which digital tools will make procurement not only more cost-effective but also more strategic.

The study showed that leaders define their own strategies for becoming digital and just take inspiration from startups, since startups typically focus on single instead of holistic solutions. However, they are willing to use solutions from startups that can be added in or taken out of their own solutions as needed.

Across the board, survey results showed that all companies have more ambition to invest in new technologies than in previous years. More than 60 percent of respondents said they would invest in digital tools, such as self-service portals, cloud computing or advanced data visualization. Leaders in procurement acknowledge that getting employee buy-in for change processes is critical to their success. This is especially needed for changes involving new digital tools or new ways of working, as people may be worried that their jobs will be replaced by a machine. Our experience shows that the most difficult part of making digital procurement work is the cultural change required to adopt and use digital tools to their full potential, along with the mindset changes that are needed when the role of a core function like procurement changes.

Becoming digital is a sweeping change that comes with many implications for processes and people. The remark, "If you want to become digital, focus on the people," holds true. Employees will need a broader view of the supply chain and different skillsets than before. And they must accept the changing role and identity of procurement. To ease the transition, we recommend:

- *Build a vision and a story:* Develop the case for change that explains why digitalization and agile organizations are needed to improve the performance of procurement.
- *Communicate:* Tell employees why change is necessary, why now, and what the ultimate goal is. Communicate this story in different ways and on different

3

channels. This might include via live meetings with Q&A, in newsletters or with apps and videos. It is also important to give employees a chance to give feedback.

— *Train*: Offer employees appropriate training on tools so that they are not overwhelmed by them, and make sure that the training is used widely.

— *Be enthusiastic about digital procurement:* Define digital projects which have a high chance of making a positive impact and let digital enthusiasts use these solutions and present those achievements to management and colleagues. Sooner or later, others will begin to wonder when they will have the chance to work with more digital tools as well.

— *Adapt to the needs of employees:* Expect that employees will have different levels of enthusiasm and knowledge about digital tools. Often this means communications should be two-pronged: One set for those who are fans of digital tools and another set of communications for doubters. Not everyone will be willing or able to adapt to the new way of working. Some may want or need to leave the procurement department.

2019 Procurement Study

In 2019, Kearney conducted a different study on digital procurement, this one with roughly 35 high-level procurement managers. The study showed that interest in digital procurement is high. Some 71 percent of procurement managers said it was their first priority. Just 10 percent haven't started looking into it yet. Most companies saw the main benefit of digital procurement as tools to make processes more efficient, for instance so that headcount can be reduced. The second most common benefit perceived was the potential to lower the company's costs by using more effective tools for procurement, followed by increasing the value-add activities for internal business partners and stakeholders.

A majority of participants (62 percent) believe that they could achieve their targets by partnering with procurement solution providers (for example SAP Ariba, Coupa, Synertrade, Oracle, Ivalua, etc.). Thirty-eight percent say they need to set up internal digital or data science departments, and a small fraction of respondents believes they can make digital procurement a reality without external help.

Nearly half of companies surveyed say that budget restrictions are a main restraint for digitalization (48 percent). Some 38 percent say that the problem is missing IT resources, while the same percent of respondents think change management is holding back digitalization. To bring the workforce up to speed, 62 percent of the participants are tackling the change management aspects and potential knowledge shortcomings by providing training and workshops, for instance in agile working methods and analytics.

A majority of participants are still working with the typical category approach (48 percent), while 33 percent are doing sprints within projects and taking agile approaches to making changes. Just some 19 percent of participants have completely reorganized procurement.

Procurement managers are clear about which new technologies will most support the digitalization of procurement. They rank AI first, followed by RPA, advanced analytics and then blockchain. We asked about the integration of the data science stack and found that the number one technology, AI, has not been widely adopted. Integration of diverse data sources was progressing though. Some 50 percent of participants had integrated ERP feeds and were storing and harmonizing big data sources. Twenty-one percent of participants said they were using analytics and AI-based tools, and 36 percent were using automation tools.

Though participants see the relevance of analytics, adoption is still low. Spend pattern analysis was common, with 72 percent of participants adopting it, whereas other applications had low uptake, including product and service specification analytics, TCO analytics and analytics for complex bidding. All of these had less than 50 percent adoption.

More than 90 percent of respondents said procurement tools were integrated with tools for sales and operations planning. Also, other standardized solutions and tools have high adoption rates, such as tendering tools (80 percent). Meanwhile, only 43 percent of respondents said they are using digital tools to manage supplier segmentations, while 36 percent had automated the tracking of supplier performance, including scorecards and historical performance. Twenty-nine percent used digital tools to capture compliance to contracts and service-level agreements, and 14 percent used them for 360° supplier risk management.

The study also showed:

- *Digital procurement is a must.* It is the number one priority of more than 70 percent of procurement professionals. There is no way around it anymore.
- *Tool implementation is not everything.* Effective digital procurement also requires the organization to adapt and people to change their mindsets.
- *Make procurement departments more effective, not just more efficient.* Done right, implementing digital procurement will enable CPOs to deliver extra savings and innovation, and it will ultimately support the company's revenue.
- *Procurement has the knowledge and ambition to make itself digital, but the practice and implementation are lacking.* AI and RPA are identified as the main technology game-changers, but few have yet implemented advanced tools. Funding and further training are needed for digital procurement to reach its full potential.

How to Embark on the Digital Procurement Journey

» Digital business transformation is not just about automating or inserting technology into an existing process. Nor is it about replacing paper or people. – Gartner

In procurement, companies have the chance to create new business designs and delivery models by using a range of digital technologies.

Procurement executives need to make digital a priority on their agenda and pursue a structured approach to rolling out digital infrastructure and the organizational changes that will be needed to make the most of digital tools.

3

When Kearney rolls out a digital procurement strategy, the steps are as follows:

- Step 1: The first step is to assess the digital maturity of the organization and if it is meeting the needed requirements. To evaluate the digital status quo and to understand where to act, procurement must take into account the corporate digital strategy and should consider the eight dimensions of the Kearney House of Purchasing and Supply. This framework provides a holistic view of all areas that CPOs are responsible for.
- Step 2: Based on what is learned, the second step is to develop a digital vision with the CPO and the leadership team, and to develop supporting initiatives to match strategy to the current state of the organization assessed in Step 1. Here it is critical to take a holistic approach to tools and processes, understanding the critical paths and specific requirements for each. This understanding will also help with prioritizing initiatives.
- Step 3: The third step is to develop a clear roadmap and prepare for implementation. The CPO needs to discuss his or her digital vision and initiatives with key stakeholders in the company. In parallel, procurement must write a high-level business case for the recommended changes. Before beginning with an implementation, companies need an implementation roadmap with clear timelines, agreed and approved investments and milestones. The roadmap should address technology, content, capabilities, organizational aspects and the rollout across functions and geographies.

Understanding Customers and Suppliers to Unlock Value

Contents

© Springer Nature Switzerland AG 2020
M. F. Strohmer et al., *Disruptive Procurement*, https://doi.org/10.1007/978-3-030-38950-5_4

The Disruptive Power of Procurement

Procurement is a relatively new discipline. In the early years, the focus was almost exclusively on lowering the prices of goods and services that were purchased. The idea was catching on just as the Communist bloc opened, and the size of the global workforce increased by one billion people. This caused labor costs to decline, and suppliers made concessions with the hopes of winning more business in a booming economy.

Today, after decades of focusing on cost reductions, customers and suppliers find themselves in a different situation. Nowadays, most procurement organizations are already running a tight ship. This makes it even more difficult to have leverage over suppliers. Companies have already analyzed supplier markets, factor costs, and competitive prices, and most have benchmarked the cost elements that are critical for providing their products and services.

But how much cost savings can procurement extract from a supplier that is already on shaky ground? And how hard can you push before suppliers compromise product quality, delivery reliability or working conditions? Furthermore, what strategies are available for increasing value while lowering costs?

To overcome the limitations of what is known as desktop procurement, seasoned professionals need to become curious and open-minded like a beginner. "In the beginner's mind there are many possibilities. In the expert's mind there are few," wrote the Zen Buddhist monk Shunryū Suzuki. We encourage procurement professionals to examine established beliefs, facilitate innovation among suppliers and hit the pavement to spend more time with suppliers.

Get Out There

Over the past 20 years working with procurement teams, we noticed how little time procurement makes available to understand the value creation processes of their suppliers. In some cases, they don't really understand the products or services they are buying. To turn this around, procurement professionals must better understand how value is created for customers and be able to articulate this.

A little bit of curiosity can go far, and there is always a way to better understand what you're buying. Grabbing a coffee and talking to engineers, marketing people, or others in your own company can work wonders. Trade journals and online courses offered by universities are also valuable sources of knowledge. Or grab a toolbox and start disassembling the product: Taking products apart with a screwdriver or wrench can become an important procurement process step.

A New Approach to Procurement

Our approach is based on two dimensions for disrupting procurement:
- "Knowledge of how suppliers create value for us" and
- "Knowledge of how we create value for customers."

4

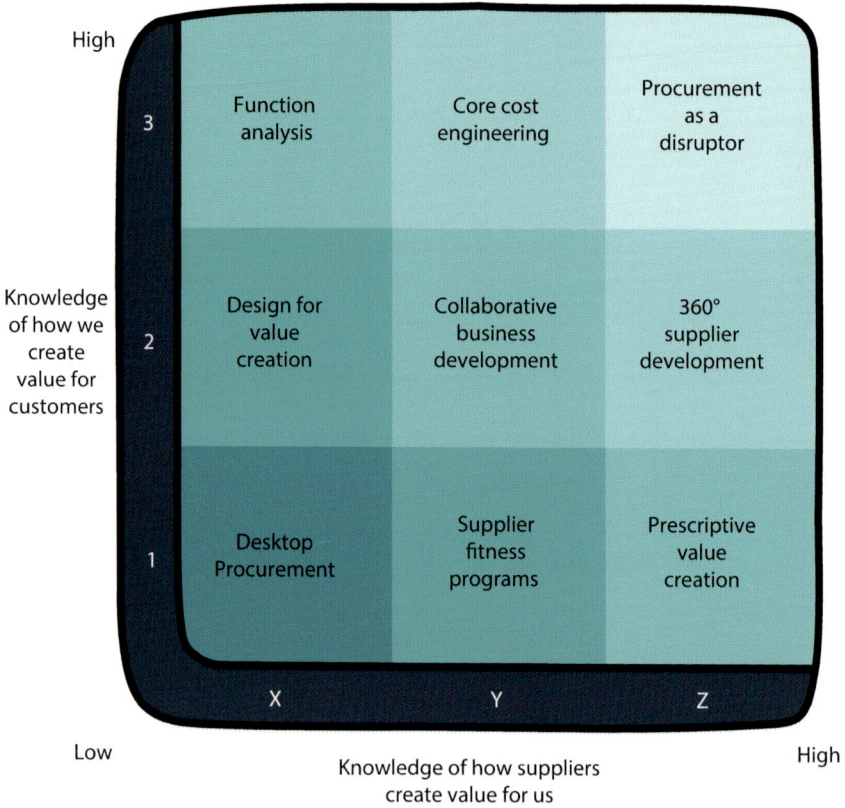

	X (Low)	**Y**	**Z** (High)
3 (High)	Function analysis	Core cost engineering	Procurement as a disruptor
2	Design for value creation	Collaborative business development	360° supplier development
1	Desktop Procurement	Supplier fitness programs	Prescriptive value creation

Knowledge of how we create value for customers (vertical axis)

Knowledge of how suppliers create value for us (horizontal axis)

Fig. 4.1 Disruptive Procurement framework

We have plotted the tools that can get a company to the point where their procurement function is a disruptor. They can be found along two axes that represent these ideas (see Fig. 4.1).

The blocks of tools build on each other, and there is no linear or prescribed path to getting to the point of being a disruptor. Companies are choosing their approach based on their depth of knowledge in these two dimensions.

Most companies begin with basic desktop procurement, which includes analyzing factor costs and competitive prices, and benchmarking various cost elements of their products and services. They then become increasingly sophisticated by adding capabilities from additional building blocks, such as a supplier fitness program or core cost engineering.

The basic assumption of the Disruptive Procurement framework is that the more you know about both axes, the more effective you will be in dealing with suppliers, and the higher the value generated by focusing on entire product or service lines.

For example:

- High knowledge about how suppliers create value for your company allows you to spot shortcomings in suppliers' value creation processes. By helping the supplier identify problems and improve on value creation processes, a procurement team helps its own organization and the other.

— Similarly, understanding how your own company creates value for its customers helps you identify products and services that have been specified to ensure performance, quality, and other considerations—but at a cost that exceeds their value to your customers.

Let us now look at the nine building blocks of the framework more closely.

Desktop Procurement

With the lifting of the Iron Curtain, labor prices declined, leading to an unprecedented period of global economic growth. Tumbling labor costs and the promise of more business gave suppliers plenty of wiggle room to make concessions on prices. During this time, desktop procurement came of age. It was characterized by creating spend categories and identifying new suppliers, and by tools such as Requests for Proposals (RFP) and online auctions. The name "desktop" was coined since all these things are typically performed from your desk.

Today, procurement professionals also analyze factor costs and competitive prices, and they benchmark the cost elements that are critical for providing their products and services. All this research—which falls under desktop procurement—is extremely important, but it doesn't always help procurement organizations to add value in break-through dimensions.

In the world of desktop procurement, much energy is poured into analyzing the spend, assessing the supply market, and developing lots of ideas to get higher savings from suppliers. In the past, this was done with homegrown spreadsheets. Today, software companies offer procurement tools for just about everything, from source-to-pay workflows and category strategy development, to idea implementation management.

With such tools, there's always one more analysis a procurement professional can do. Many end up spending most of their time looking at their screens and not really understanding the business or finding innovative ways to support it. Essentially, desktop procurement doesn't help companies have meaningful results in a low-growth environment. At best, it helps deliver some savings; in the worst case, too much price pressure can lead suppliers to cut corners.

There are dozens of examples of suppliers using the wrong or poor-grade materials and resorting to unacceptable practices, such as unsafe working conditions or child labor, due to the price pressure they feel from their customers. A less visible but equally dangerous way of cutting corners is for a supplier to stop investing in the future because their profit margins are so small. That's risky because suppliers are an important source of innovation.

Today's desktop procurement is, of course, digital. New collaborative tools make the lives of procurement professionals easier, artificial intelligence (AI) supports RFQs, and comprehensive benchmark data is available. In general, the digitalization of desktop procurement is an extremely important basis for more advanced approaches to disrupting with procurement. But, in the end, it is still desktop procurement, even if it's digital.

Adding Value in Break-Through Dimensions

Success factors include:

- Category tree and spend cube processes in place to provide full transparency of external expenditures by category, location and supplier
- Supplier market dynamics: Detailed understanding and analyses regarding growth, competition level, cost drivers, and the M&A activity of your suppliers is necessary.
- A gated strategic sourcing process with differentiated strategies by category helps with internal alignment.
- Experience with different approaches for competitive supplier negotiations: For desktop procurement, advanced negotiation skills are important. This includes an understanding of game theory-based negotiations.
- Strong analytical capabilities
- Automated processes wherever feasible

Example: Value Capture for a Construction Equipment Maker

A global construction equipment maker decided it was high time to stop acting as a financial holding company and start reaping operational synergies from its portfolio of businesses. The corporation consisted of six divisions and more than 50 individual companies spread across the globe. Its independent mid-sized companies spent billions of dollars instead of acting as a multi-billion-dollar corporation. The company was looking for transformational savings instead of small incremental savings, and it decided to start its journey towards operations integration with a large-scale global strategic sourcing project. The project was driven by desktop procurement but still led to double-digit savings.

First, the company analyzed the "as is" situation. It identified who buys what from whom and built a spend cube. It also identified savings potential, defined three sourcing waves and prioritized its activities.

In a next step, the company started broad communication to the supply market. It sent more than 2,000 letters to its current suppliers and invited more than 20,000 new suppliers to participate in the project and start engaging with its procurement department. This whole communication process was purely desktop driven – identifying the right suppliers through research, sending communication, keeping track of the status of each individual supplier, and communicating with suppliers by email, phone, etc.

In the following step, the actual sourcing wave was started. The company focused on its biggest spend categories – steel, steel components, cylinders and hydraulic components. It also started a large-scale RFP process with bidding sheets with up to 1,000 articles, sites where suppliers could download drawings, and help desk phone numbers and emails to support suppliers in the process.

Twenty years ago, these processes would have been supported by fax machines. Today, these processes are supported with highly efficient online tools or AI-based tools. And while the RFI/RFP process has become more and more efficient, it is still simple desktop procurement. It is important, powerful and delivers results. But it is best seen as a foundation for building blocks that can lead to disruption.

Supplier Fitness Programs

Fitness is just as important for a supplier partnering up with a customer as it is for all of us in our daily lives. In sports, fitness programs help you burn fat, build muscle and get in shape. Many people use a personal trainer to find an individual approach.

The same is also true of a supplier fitness program, which is designed to find the right ways to identify and implement cost reductions and help suppliers become more competitive.

Implementing a supplier fitness program is the logical next step after a company has a good desktop procurement system in place. Usually, supplier fitness programs focus on helping existing large suppliers improve their own cost position through a structured program. Programs typically have the following phases:

— *Preparation and selection phase:* First, appropriate suppliers need to be chosen for the program. Companies cannot offer supplier fitness programs for all suppliers. Consider how complex that would be for an industrial company with some 8,000 group suppliers. Then category-specific questionnaires need to be created, and companies should conduct internal and external analyses of benchmark data for products, services and processes. At the same time, companies should visit suppliers to gain an understanding of the supplier's entire cost structure and product portfolio.

— *Opportunity scan phase:* Now it's time to evaluate the supplier, initially by analyzing its processes, with a particular focus on procurement and production. After identifying cost-cutting potential, companies can help suppliers identify concrete activities that can boost the supplier's fitness. These need to be defined, reviewed and recorded.

— *Implementation phase:* Supplier fitness measures can then be implemented in close collaboration between the supplier and the customer, initially in a pilot project. If all goes well, the pilot can then be successively extended throughout the supplier's operation.

— *Reporting phase:* Companies must constantly review implementation results and the consistency of implementation.

Reducing Costs and Helping Suppliers Become More Competitive

Success factors include:

- *In-depth expertise on value creation/production processes:* In order to support and consult the supplier in improving the value creation process, companies need a deep and profound knowledge of production techniques. This knowledge may come from inhouse, from selected manufacturing engineers or from specialized consultants. Earning credibility with the supplier is key.
- *Strong communication skills on all levels:* A supplier fitness program normally involves contact with several departments at the supplier. This includes contact with top management, who needs to agree on the program, in controlling, the source of key data, and in manufacturing, where companies can get more data and understand production. The benefits of such a program need to be communicated clearly within the supplier's organization. This is not an easy job, since companies may be proud of their capabilities and not willing to get outside help.
- *Persistency:* Once the supplier fitness program has been conducted and suppliers have committed to certain actions, it is important to track the measures implemented and their effectiveness.

And what about tools in this case?

In many ways, we are skeptical about how tools can end up taking on a life of their own in a pure desktop procurement approach. To be clear, we are not opposed to using analytical tools—quite the contrary. What we advocate is the smart deployment of the right tools that tap into the right data sets. Big data analytics and industry 4.0 concepts are the foundational pillars of many of the most powerful supplier fitness programs. Integrating suppliers' suppliers into an ecosystem and helping them to implement tools such as predictive maintenance will be of value.

Example: The Automotive Industry – Where It All Started

If you look back at Opel's original 1985 global sourcing project, you see what its instigator Ignacio López did after the first cost reduction rounds with suppliers. He took a team of seasoned manufacturing professionals and had them spend quality time in the factories of suppliers. They analyzed production processes in detail, identified shortcomings, and helped suppliers increase their efficiency. The resulting savings were shared between the supplier and Opel. The automotive industry has embraced this approach enthusiastically. Toyota is the shining example in this regard and has a highly structured program in place to ensure that all its suppliers are fully compatible with its Toyota Production System (TPS).

We are not suggesting that every company develop its own version of TPS. What is recommended, though, is that category managers go out to their suppliers, understand their value creation processes, and guide them in conducting programs to cut costs, reduce inventories and improve quality.

Example: Third-Party Manufacturing in Pharma – Providing Competitive Advantage for Suppliers

Pharmaceutical companies cannot change their suppliers as easily as other companies, due to the large number of regulations in the industry, and suppliers know this. Therefore, supplier fitness programs are an important way in the pharmaceuticals industry to find improvements without switching suppliers.

A major pharmaceutical company in Europe started a procurement transformation program in the direct and indirect spend categories. In one of its largest spend areas, business with Contract Manufacturing Organizations (CMO), it was particularly hard to achieve savings, so the company sought to improve the fitness of its main CMO suppliers.

It took a two-phase approach in which the company diagnosed CMO fitness and measured the CMO against benchmarks for production efficiency. This allowed the pharma company to develop preliminary hypotheses and identify potential areas of operational improvement for individual CMOs. It took a close look at suppliers' operational utilization, overhead costs, organizational setups, and external spend. As it turned out, some of its CMOs were significantly below the median performance score.

At the same time, suppliers went through a two-day onsite analysis. The pharma company was able to confirm and refine some of its initial hypotheses, while discarding others. For example, after one site visit, the company concluded that its provider's facility had low overall production performance and unfavorable workplace and work-cell design; non-value-adding overhead in the areas of maintenance and quality; and improvement potential in select procurement categories (for example, folding cartons).

The company helped the provider improve production performance and set up new commercial terms. Both the supplier and the client company shared the efficiency gains jointly. After the first full year, the client company saved substantially in an environment that usually has very limited savings potential.

Prescriptive Value Creation

Prescriptive value creation takes knowledge of supplier value creation to the extreme. Let's remember, high levels of knowledge about how suppliers create value for your company allows you to spot shortcomings in suppliers' value creation processes. Acquiring and applying this knowledge involves several steps.

The first is seeing many suppliers and taking what is good at one supplier and applying it to the others. Be careful, though, because sometimes entire industry clusters suffer from similar performance issues—issues grounded in practices that were perceived to be good because everybody followed them.

Bringing in insights from other industries can help overcome this. For example, asking "How would Toyota produce this part?" is always a good idea when it comes to discrete manufacturing. Helping the supplier identify and realize opportunities in its value creation processes opens new chapters in the relationship that can lead to savings and other benefits.

A common form of prescriptive value creation is outsourcing. A company deems certain elements of its operations no longer core and looks for a third party that is suited to host those operations. Suitability often just means that the third party is located in the right region with the right labor costs. The third party does not necessarily need to have concrete experience, provided it has the required managerial skills to deliver on new challenges. In these cases, the value creation processes are wholly prescribed by the customer. Essentially, the customer goes beyond product definition and actively defines the operations processes (for example materials, manufacturing, assembly, logistics) at the supplier. It understands the value creation perfectly well – often much better than the supplier itself – and simply contracts another supplier to do exactly what is required.

Spotting Shortcomings in Suppliers' Value Creation

Success factors include:
- In-depth expertise on value creation/production processes: In order to be able to prescribe value creation processes to the supplier, companies need a superior knowledge of production techniques. This may come from inhouse, with selected manufacturing engineers, or from specialized consultants. Earning credibility at the supplier is key.
- Understanding of new technologies: Companies need superior knowledge of production processes, as well as a deep and comprehensive understanding of new and different technologies.
- Adaptable suppliers: Suppliers may be too proud to accept directions on their own value creation process from a customer, or they simply doubt the expertise of the customer. Therefore, it is important to select suppliers that are adaptable and accept a certain level of customer prescription.
- Strong communication skills on all levels: Communication is key for convincing suppliers of the advantages of a prescribed value creation process.

Example: Apple's Understanding of How Suppliers Create Value
When Apple develops a new product such as the iPhone, it does not stop at industrial design and product architecture, as many of its high-tech competitors do. Instead, Apple takes a broader view that encompasses which materials to use, how to work with those materials, how to assemble the product, and how to prepare it for shipment to the end customer.

When working on the outside casing for its MacBooks and iPads, Apple determined that a technology previously applied to a relatively small series of high-precision components, computer numerical control (CNC) machining, is the perfect way to make a chassis. Apple's internal labs got the technology ready for mass production, and the company ended up buying most of the CNC machining equipment made globally between 2010 and 2012. These machines are now installed in the Chinese factories of the Taiwanese electronics contract manufacturing company Foxconn, and other Taiwanese suppliers, which are responsible for operating them. In other words, Apple enabled its suppliers to create value for Apple.

Design for Value Creation

Design for value creation requires disciplined thinking – to understand how value is created for customers. It is not enough to just define an element of a product or service that can compete successfully in the market. Rather, the product or service must also be specified in a way that suppliers say they can deliver it efficiently and effectively.

Design for value creation is a two-way street. The supplier must be forthcoming about its core competencies but also about areas that are outside of its core competencies. A supplier that is too hungry for business may grab whatever it can get and push itself into a corner. At the same time, the customer needs to listen to the supplier. And this listening process must start long before business is actually awarded. Ideally, suppliers will get on board when a company is in the concept-development stage with a new product – for example, when specifications are still fluid.

Design for value creation is not a new concept, but it has become much more sophisticated with the availability of big data and the possibility to optimize for multiple variables. The approach should be very structured and conducted across functions. It should include concept briefings and data reviews, as well as parameter definition and alignment, for instance with teams with representatives from finance, procurement, legal, engineering, marketing and others. Then companies need to model the setup and prepare for data entry – for example, they must discuss and validate the logic of the design model, with all its functions. That is followed by scenario development and assessment, which includes evaluating and challenging the capabilities of suppliers. Next is scenario modelling of results and the capture of the primary conclusions – for example with customers. Finally, it's time for a decision and implementation. Normally, top management makes the final decisions about product or service design, which is accepted by stakeholders as the best-possible solution, taking all parameters into account.

Understanding How Value is Created for Customers

Success factors include:
- *Deep insights into the core competencies of suppliers:* Reading a supplier's advertising or hearing presentations isn't enough for deep understanding. By creating a culture of openness with suppliers, they are more likely to say what they can and cannot do. The closer the collaboration, the easier it is to evaluate these capabilities.

4

— *Strong analytical skills and sophisticated tools:* Companies that want to optimize design for value creation, for instance for large-scale CAPEX projects with thousands of parameters, need people with highly specialized skills, such as the ability to optimize software. Professionals need to think about the final output and draw on specialized knowledge about product and service design to set up these complex models.

— *Experience with big data and large-scale optimization engines:* Once all parameters have been defined, the handling of big data is the next challenge. The data used must be formatted appropriately. If it has gaps, companies need to close those gaps with extrapolations or assumptions, in order to have a stable model.

— *Cross-functional collaboration:* Design for value creation is always cross-functional. R&D, manufacturing, finance, planning, procurement, marketing and others need to participate so that all different points of view are heard and considered in the design.

The following example makes the key goals of stakeholders apparent, as well as how those goals might be in conflict.

Example: Construction of a Gas Pipeline

An area where design for value creation is extremely powerful is in large CAPEX projects – for example, a gas pipeline project. Normally, procurement's job is to improve on price, quality and time. A large-scale CAPEX project, however, requires much broader thinking. Sourcing the pipeline itself seems straightforward — companies mainly need construction work, tubes and compressors. But getting the overall setup right is more difficult: The pipeline may be built in different countries, with different laws and different levels of governmental support. And the construction work will take several years, during which prices can fluctuate considerably. At an oil & gas company, a cross-functional task force from engineering, procurement and finance teamed up with a specialized analytics group to find the best approach in each area. Each of these internal stakeholders had very clear objectives to meet in the project, including some that were potentially in conflict:

Procurement wanted to:

— Define a procurement strategy that meets the requirements of the departments and shareholders

— Ensure a competitive tendering process to achieve the lowest total lifecycle cost (CAPEX, OPEX and financing costs)

— Ensure a realistic timeline for tendering, contract awards, financing, delivery and construction

— Reduce claim risk on construction and maintain the ability to incentivize suppliers

Finance wanted to:
- Achieve high Export Credit Agency (ECA) funding and ensure the liquidity of the project and to consider ECA lead time requirements
- Simulate different scenarios regarding the ECA coverage to demonstrate the impact of achieving higher or lower ECA coverage
- Break down costs to countries and steps of the value chain to maximize ECA coverage

Engineering wanted to:
- Choose suppliers/contractors who could guarantee technical requirements, system uniformity and pipeline integrity
- Choose the right number of suppliers: Ideally, it would be one, but a maximum of two compressor suppliers, and a single supplier for the compressor control rooms
- Consider financial and technical capabilities of suppliers/contractors to determine the right size of the contract

Legal wanted to:
- Ensure a competitive tendering process to meet the spirit of the EU utility tender procurement directive
- Ensure local content (for example buying) in each country
- Evaluate the different scenarios regarding liability/risk exposure (including ECAs)

Project management wanted:
- A maximum number of 15 engineering, procurement and construction (EPC) contractors to ensure the integrity of the pipeline – for example health, safety, environment, quality, budget and technical requirements
- To split the pipeline into 50 to100 kilometer sections to make it manageable
- Construction time to be assumed to be four years, with 10–12 sections constructed each year

Looking at these lists, the things each department wanted that could come into conflict with each other were: CAPEX costs, ECA coverage, liability coverage, local content, technical requirements, contracting and interfaces.

The company had to evaluate thousands of different combinations of parameters and come up with the "best design" for the overall structure by understanding how value is generated for customers and listening to suppliers about what was possible. By doing this exercise, the company significantly reduced the planned time to build the pipeline and the planned costs, something that is quite unique for large CAPEX projects.

4

> **Example: Apple Products and Design for Value Creation**
> Apple is a leader in design for value creation and doing it quickly. Consider the iPhone or iPad. Apple focused on what matters for customers as well as design, connectivity, functions and features. It wanted devices that are lightweight, had the right screen brightness, a good look and feel, appealing packaging and more. At Apple, engineers, marketing, customer experience experts and procurement typically work together to fulfill customer needs, bringing in their experience about what the customer values and how suppliers bring value.

Collaborative Business Development

When a customer and a supplier are engaged in a long-term relationship, procurement usually has an OPEX team which spends substantial time at the supplier's site to support them in making improvements on their part of the value-creation processes. Essentially, they are running a supplier fitness program with the supplier's manufacturing department, its engineering department or the supplier's own procurement department to teach the supplier more about what the buyer needs and best-practices in procurement.

At the same time, procurement is likely to be working with both suppliers and other functions at its own company, such as product development, marketing, market research and others, to collaboratively define optimal specifications. Those definitions are based on an understanding of what the customer wants, the product's core functions and market demands. In some cases, a customer will design its products and services in a way that matches the supplier's competencies, as the customer and supplier work collaboratively to define new, innovative products or services.

When the customer and the supplier work together to define new, breakthrough products or services and collaboratively launch innovative products, while sharing the rewards, we call this collaborative business development.

Working Together to Define Optimal Specifications

Success factors include:

- *Deep insights into the core competencies of suppliers:* Reading a supplier's advertising or hearing presentations isn't enough for deep understanding. By creating a culture of openness with suppliers, they are more likely to say what they can and cannot do. The closer the collaboration, the easier it is to evaluate these capabilities.
- *In-depth expertise on value creation/production processes:* In order to support and consult the supplier in improving the value creation process, companies need a deep and profound knowledge of production techniques. This knowledge may

come from inhouse from selected manufacturing engineers or from specialized consultants. Earning credibility with the supplier is key.

- *Strong communication skills on all levels:* A collaborative business development program normally involves contact with several departments at the supplier. This includes contact with top management, who needs to agree on the program, in controlling, the source of key data, and in manufacturing, where companies can get more data and understand production. The benefits of such a program need to be communicated clearly within the supplier's organization. This is not an easy job, since companies may be proud of their capabilities and not willing to get outside help.
- *Persistency:* Once all parameters have been defined, the handling of big data is the next challenge. The data used must be formatted appropriately. If it has gaps, companies need to close them with extrapolations or assumptions, in order to have a stable model.
- *Open-mindedness and readiness to change:* An important pre-requisite to collaborative business development is readiness to change.
- *Cross-functional collaboration:* Collaborative business development is always cross functional. R&D, manufacturing, finance, planning, procurement, marketing and others need to participate so that all different points of view are heard and considered in the design.

Example: The Daimler-Bosch Relationship

Daimler and Robert Bosch have a customer-supplier relationship that reaches back more than a century. Both are headquartered in the Stuttgart region, and both share a similar commitment to innovation and excellence. Over time, the product lifecycles of both companies have largely converged. Daimler's Mercedes-Benz S-class cars routinely launch with brand-new Robert Bosch technology as a showcase for what can be done. Later, these technologies get used in other Daimler car lines and by other carmakers. The strong alignment of product lifecycles and product launches has greatly benefited both companies. Many of Bosch's products would not have materialized without Daimler as a launch customer, and Daimler's success can hardly be imagined without Bosch's technologies.

360° Supplier Development

Short of acquiring a supplier, 360° supplier development is the most immersive way for a customer to interact with its supplier. Rather than focusing on particular aspects of the supplier's value creation process and product or service design, the supplier's entire business enters into the scope. Elements covered include the customer-supplier interface (activities often referred to as Supplier Relationship Management (SRM) and Customer Relationship Management (CRM)), as well as the supplier's R&D, procurement, operations (for example, its factories), and its overall product or service architecture. The ultimate objective of 360° supplier development is to have closer relationships with fewer suppliers. This will benefit all parties involved. In addition, the:

- Buyer will spend more quality time with suppliers
- Suppliers will get higher spend from the buyer
- Buyer will have a higher mindshare with supplier executives

4

360° supplier development typically starts with communication to suppliers that there are far too many suppliers, and savings targets are not being reached. Companies then express that the supply base needs to be consolidated to include the most competitive suppliers. The suppliers that "opt in" and choose to commit to accelerated cost reductions are supported throughout the process to further increase competitiveness in important areas. These include:

- *Manufacturing excellence* – Driving lean principles across factory ecosystems including those in direct labor and support labor costs
- *Purchasing excellence* – Fully capturing cost savings opportunities with sub-tier suppliers and ensuring that these are passed through
- *Specification improvement* – There is room for improvement both at an incremental specification level and regarding the overall product architecture.

Manufacturing excellence   Suppliers are expected to ensure lean principles across their entire factory ecosystem. Some typical areas of improvement are Overall Equipment Effectiveness, line balance, work content, visualization and transparency, and Total Productive Maintenance (TPM).

Purchasing excellence   Suppliers are expected to introduce state-of-the-art tools like the Purchasing Chessboard®. The Purchasing Chessboard® is inspired by the logic of supply power and demand power—a concept that governed the dynamics in the bazaars of Babylon, helped Venice rise to greatness and formed the basis of the British Empire.

The idea is that any sourcing category can be plotted along those two dimensions of supply and demand power. And depending on the power balance, very different basic strategies to reduce cost or generate value apply. They are:

- Leverage competition among suppliers
- Seek joint advantage with supplier
- Change nature of demand
- Manage spend

These four basic strategies can be detailed into many additional value-adding approaches that suppliers should excel in and apply.

Specification improvement   Suppliers are also expected to help improve product specifications. Working through prepared logic trees can help structure the thinking towards incremental specification improvements. An example would be a logic tree for potential material changes or design changes (see ◘ Figs. 4.2 and 4.3).

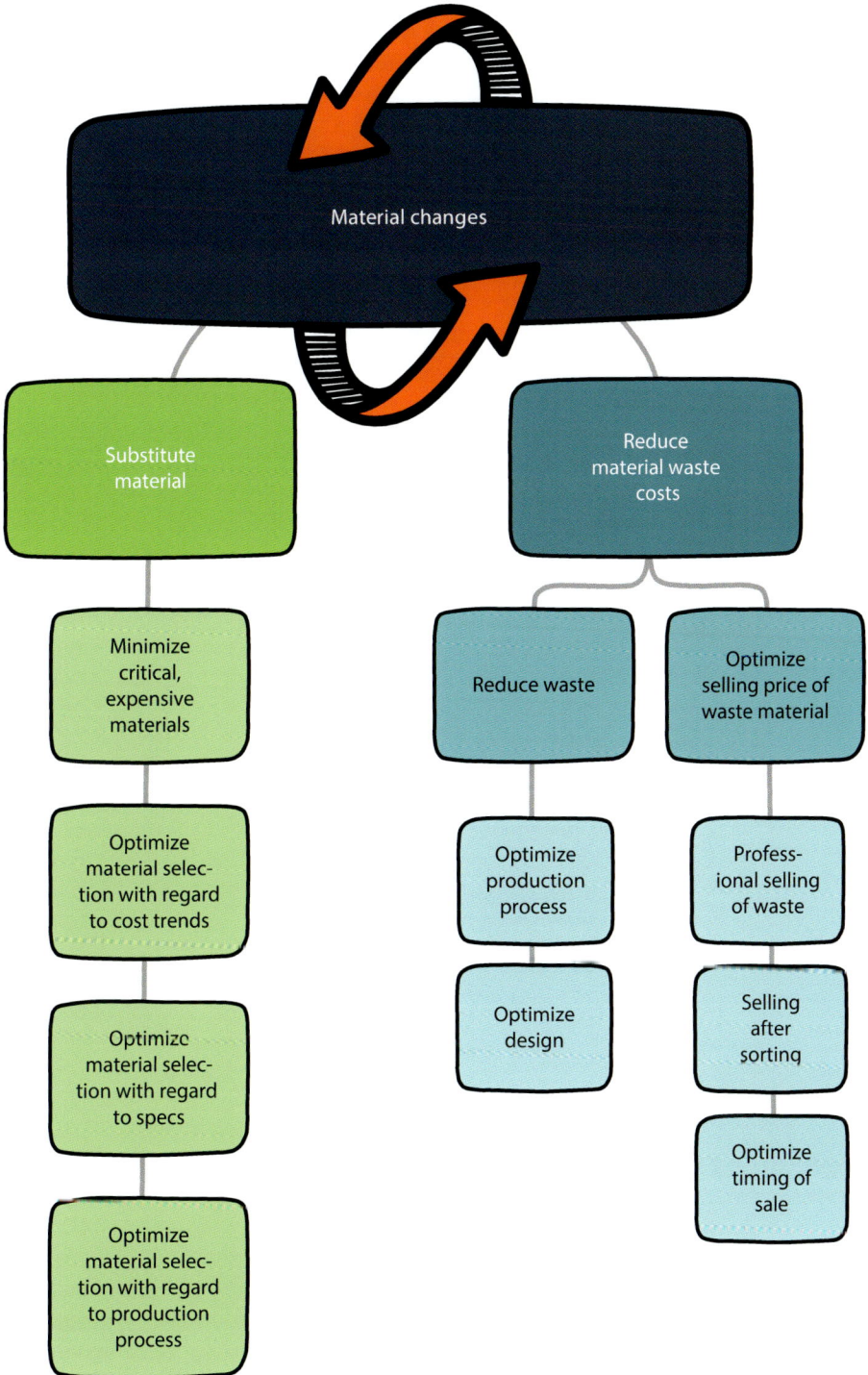

● **Fig. 4.2** Logic tree for materials changes

4

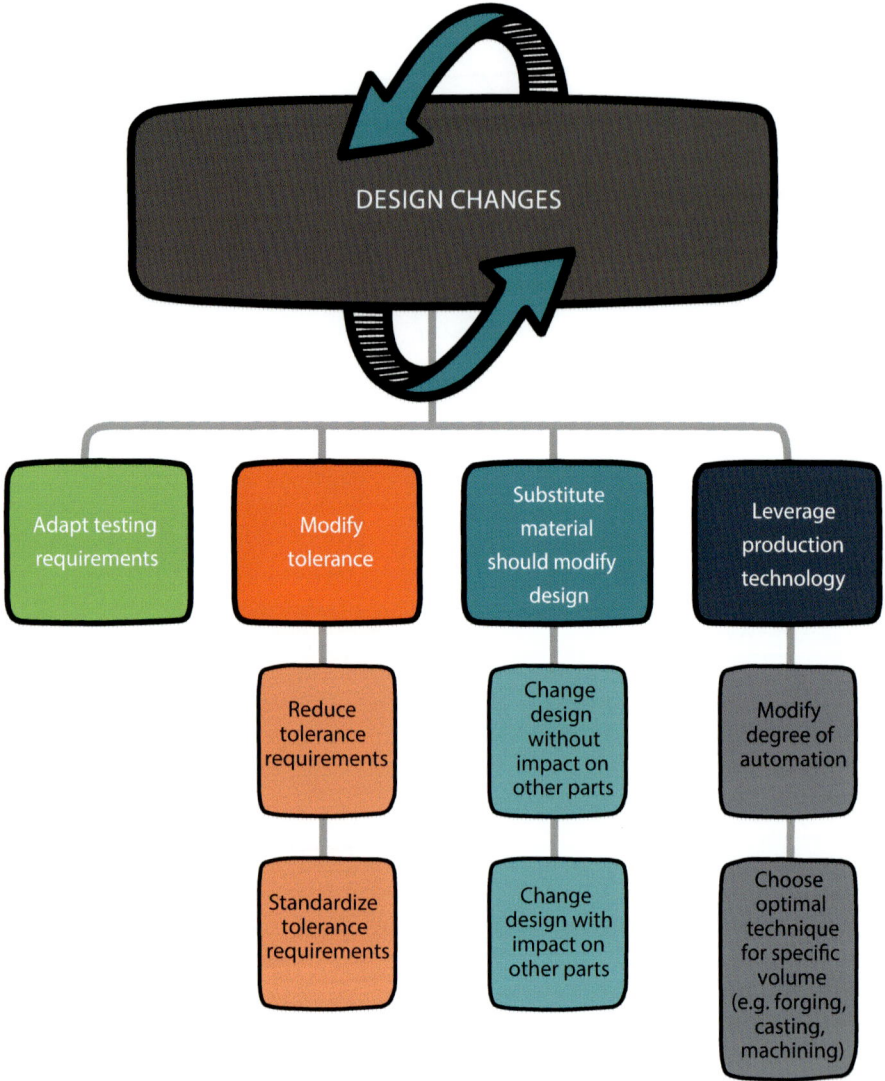

❑ **Fig. 4.3** Logic tree for design changes

Developing Closer Relationships with Fewer Suppliers

Success factors include:

- *Deep insights into the core competencies of suppliers:* Reading a supplier's advertising or hearing presentations isn't enough for deep understanding. By creating a culture of openness with suppliers, they are more likely to say what they can and cannot do. The closer the collaboration, the easier it is to evaluate these capabilities.

- *In-depth expertise on value creation/production processes:* In order to support and consult the supplier in improving the value creation process, companies need a deep and profound knowledge of production techniques. This knowledge may come from inhouse from selected manufacturing engineers or from specialized consultants. Earning credibility with the supplier is key.
- *Strong communication skills on all levels:* A 360° supplier development program normally involves contact with several departments at the supplier. This includes contact with top management, who needs to agree on the program, in controlling, the source of key data, and in manufacturing, where companies can get more data and understand production. The benefits of such a program need to be communicated clearly within the supplier's organization. This is not an easy job, since companies may be proud of their capabilities and not willing to get outside help.
- *Open-mindedness and readiness to change:* An important pre-requisite to 360° supplier development is readiness to change.
- *Cross-functional collaboration:* 360° supplier development is always cross functional. R&D, manufacturing, finance, planning, procurement, marketing and others need to participate so that all different points of view are heard and considered in the design.

Example: Unilever and Frozen Food in Austria

In the early 1960s, Unilever moved into the Austrian frozen food market. First, it built a giant frozen food warehouse on the outskirts of Vienna. Since the distance from harvest to the frozen food warehouse needed to be as short as possible to ensure product quality, Unilever recruited local farmers to grow peas, spinach and other vegetables. By deploying a massive program to introduce modern agricultural techniques to those farmers, Unilever managed to transform a traditional farming region into a highly productive, specialized cluster of industrialized vegetable farms—without changing the established ownership structures.

Example: PC Makers and 360° Supplier Development

Recently, makers of personal computers (PCs) began using 360° supplier development to make their suppliers more competitive, given sluggish growth and rising labor costs in China, where much of the production is located. At the beginning of China's industrialization, labor was available at basically an irrelevant cost. As a result, millions of Chinese workers were employed doing completely inefficient manufacturing processes. And due to the low cost of labor, those inefficiencies did not matter. With labor cost rising to significantly higher levels in the meantime, China's still inefficient manufacturing processes mean "Made in China" has lost some of its competitive edge. Companies have huge improvement opportunities. For many PC makers, 360° supplier development is becoming a matter of survival.

Function Analysis

Traditional cost-reduction techniques begin with the question: "How can we reduce the cost of an item?" or "How can I do that for less?"

In both cases, the questions are directly focused on how to reduce costs without really understanding the inherent function of the item or process. This lack of knowledge keeps procurement professionals from correctly judging the item's value, which usually leads to inflated prices.

Function analysis is the act of defining the relative cost of the discrete functions of a product and identifying those with disproportionate costs. It determines whether any functions can be eliminated without significantly degrading the usefulness of the product. In function analysis, the first question is "What does it do?" Procurement professionals start with a breakdown of the product or service into discrete elements. For each of these elements, the functions are listed and expressed in verb-object pairs consisting of active verbs and quantifiable nouns.

For example, the functions of a mounting bracket are "to support load" and "attach part." Each function is then classified into two "buckets"—the useful bucket (such as "support load") and the harmful bucket (for example, "adds weight").

Then the cost of the product or service is allocated to the different parts or components of the product/service and to the different functions that each part or component plays. Establishing cost-to-function relationships is important for identifying ways to improve the product or service. By identifying elements of the product or services with unfavorable cost-benefit ratios, procurement professionals can see where to "attack" costs. Often, the most straightforward way to reduce costs is to simply eliminate elements with high cost and harmful functions. Of course, this only works when remaining elements can somehow do the same as the element that was eliminated. To do this in manufacturing, scientists must often be called in; in service industries, it requires raw creativity.

Function analysis is a five-step process which is typically performed in a workshop environment. The time required varies, depending on the complexity of the product and the scope of the workshop.

- *Step 1: Identification of function.* The first step is to break down the product into sub-assemblies or sub-systems and to identify the functions of each sub-assembly or sub-system.
- *Step 2: Naming of the functions.* Next, all the functions identified need to be given a meaningful name. This should consist of two expressive words: an active verb and a measurable noun, which together clearly illustrate and define the significance of the individual components. Examples would be "Prevents corrosion," "Positions parts," or "Absorbs vibration."
- *Step 3: Classification of functions.* The functions are assigned to one of four classes: basic, critical, supporting and non-supporting.
  - *Basic functions* are the specific work that the product was designed to do. A test for basic functions is asking the question, "If this function were removed, would the purpose of the product still be fulfilled?" For example, a car door

hinge must support weight, close the door and resist impact. If the hinge were removed, could these purposes be fulfilled?

- *Critical functions* are those which are required to make the basic functions happen. They are the designers' choice of means to accomplish the basic functions.
- *Supporting functions* are those which make the critical functions happen better, faster, longer etc., for example, a switch in an electrical socket protects against power surges.
- *Non-supporting functions* are any other functions defined within the system that have no effect on the basic function of the product. This may include functions which we want (and are willing to pay for) from a part but are totally unrelated to the basic function of the part or service.

- Classifying each function will provide greater insight for the team to identify cost reduction opportunities. For example, what does an exhaust hanger do?
    - *"Supports weight"* is a basic function – the primary function provided by the product
    - *"Positions parts"* is a critical function – without this function the product will not work
    - *"Absorbs vibration"* is a supporting function which helps the product perform better
    - *"Regulates motion"* is also a supporting function
    - *"Resists corrosion"* is a non-supporting function that does not affect the performance of the product much

- *Step 4: Valuation of cost-function ratios.* This step is essential for identifying potential improvements. The information is listed on an evaluation sheet along with all components and their functions. On each individual line, the relationship between part, function and cost is valued. Adding up all the columns produces total costs.

- *Step 5: Identification of potential improvements.* The following are general rules for identifying components to optimize:
    - The product can be viewed as cost-effective if the costs predominantly occur in the area of basic or critical functions.
    - If significant costs are found in supporting functions, savings can be achieved without changing the basic concept.
    - The highest savings can be realized in non-supporting functions.

Defining the Relative Costs of Discrete Functions

Success factors include:

- *Deep insights into the core competencies of suppliers:* Reading a supplier's advertising or hearing presentations isn't enough for deep understanding. By creating a culture of openness with suppliers, they are more likely to say what they can and cannot do. The closer the collaboration, the easier it is to evaluate these capabilities.

- *In-depth expertise on value creation/production processes:* In order to support and consult the supplier in improving the value creation process, companies need a deep and profound knowledge of production techniques. This knowledge may come from inhouse from selected manufacturing engineers or from specialized consultants. Earning credibility with the supplier is key.
- *Strong analytical skills and sophisticated tools:* Companies that want to optimize design for value creation, for instance for large-scale CAPEX projects with thousands of parameters, need people with highly specialized skills, such as the ability to optimize software. Professionals need to think about the final output and draw on specialized knowledge about product and service design to set up these complex models.
- *Experience with big data and large-scale optimization engines:* Once all parameters have been defined, the handling of data is the next challenge. The data used must be formatted appropriately. If it has gaps, companies need to close them with extrapolations or assumptions, in order to have a stable model.
- *An accurate, up-to-date, and costed Bill of Materials (BOM):* Function analysis is also about correctly allocating costs to components and functions, therefore an accurate and up-to-date BOM is important.
- *The right people who can follow the methodology correctly:* Doing function analysis takes diligence and people with experience in following processes.

Example: Function Analysis at Samsung

Samsung began using a type of function analysis in the early 2000s that was inspired by Uzbekistan-born inventor Genrich Altshuller around 1950. Altshuller's disciples used the Theory of Inventive Problem Solving (often referred to by its Russian acronym TRIZ) in the aerospace and defense sector. The theory was one reason the Soviet Union was able to keep up the space and arms race for decades at only a fraction of the budget available to the United States. Samsung is said to have hired groups of scientists and engineers trained in TRIZ to help it come up with its own unique designs and become a global consumer electronics brand.

Example: Circumventing a Patent Using Function Analysis

Function analyses not only help save costs, they also help companies find completely new technical solutions. Within the scope of a procurement project at a European machinery production company, the team and the procurement director discussed whether component A should be included in the scope of the project. The procurement director advised caution: "It would be better to leave it alone. To my knowledge, the supplier has applied for patents for component A in Europe, Japan, and North America." So far, that didn't really matter because the company only needed component A for one small-volume product. However, the sales figures for this product had risen sharply, and the latest market forecasts indicated even stronger growth in the coming year. That would mean the company would become increasingly dependent on that one supplier, so it decided to take action to prevent that.

The team carried out a functional analysis on component A, identified its drawbacks, and developed a new and better technical approach. The functional analysis was complete, and the team of Russian scientists that conducted it were able to find no fewer than 53 drawbacks in component A.

Shortly thereafter, the team came up with 20 alternative designs to the current design which fulfilled the following criteria:
- Financially and technically feasible
- Did not infringe the pending patent for component A
- Included some considerable improvements compared to component A
- Component was patentable

Presenting these alternatives in renegotiations with the existing supplier could give the buyer an advantage.

Core Cost Engineering

Talking about the core of something means to focus on what is the most important part and to leave anything else out that does not count as the core. Think about core competencies or core business or core products of companies.

Similarly, core cost engineering takes away layers upon layers of ancillary functions that have piled up on products and services and examines the core function that the customer really expects. Then it looks for the most efficient way to perform this function and, finally, it adds minimal extra functions that are required to be able to actually sell the product or add something that the client or consumer is ready to pay for.

To get it right, companies must understand consumer needs and know how suppliers create value around the core cost elements. The approach is straight forward:
- *Step 1: Analyze what the customer really expects.* The starting point for a core cost engineering approach is a blank sheet of paper and pen to write down clearly what the customer is expecting from a certain product. Cars exist, for example, to bring people from one place to the next, regardless of the weather. Articulating the real customer expectation should be a cross-functional exercise so that expectations are not skewed toward the experience of a particular department. Marketing, for instance, would probably describe broad expectations of the product or include "nice to haves."
- *Step 2: Benchmark against competitor products – especially "ruthless" competitors.* Looking at a broad range of competitor products always brings new perspectives into play. Here, the most important step is to define the right competitor that can serve as a benchmark for fulfilling the core expectations of

the customer. Sometimes, these products already exist. Think of the cheapest smartphone, which is below 5 dollars, or the Tata Nano car which cost 1,440 euros for a four-seater for a while. The Bajaj Qute cost even less, but it was not intended as a four-seater. If you are not able to benchmark, ask the question: How would a competitor in a greenfield environment with the best manufacturing and supporting processes, for example, access to sourcing markets, build the product?

- *Step 3: Challenge. Challenge. Challenge.* Benchmarking is good but only the beginning of the process. Companies can also ask if this is already everything they can do? Is the competitor product really the benchmark? Second, it is important to adapt the "greenfield ruthless competitor" approach to the supplier's capabilities by constantly asking how the supplier can operate at close to the cost structure of a greenfield company.
- *Step 4: Go beyond the core when necessary.* Add those product components that are necessary to sell the product, even if they do not contribute to the core. One example is adding a housing for an electronic device.
- *Step 5: Fine-tune the product* with elements that the customer is ready to pay for that go over and beyond those identified in Step 4. Think about the list of extras consumers can choose from when ordering a car. The goal in this step is to increase the margin that can be earned on a product.

Knowing How Suppliers Create Value Around Core Cost Elements

Success factors include:
- *Deep insights into the core competencies of suppliers:* Reading a supplier's advertising or hearing presentations isn't enough for deep understanding. By creating a culture of openness with suppliers, they are more likely to say what they can and cannot do. The closer the collaboration, the easier it is to evaluate these capabilities.
- *In-depth expertise on value creation/production processes:* In order to support the supplier and consult the supplier in improving the value creation process, companies need a deep and profound knowledge of production techniques. This knowledge may come from inhouse from selected manufacturing engineers or from specialized consultants. Earning credibility with the supplier is key.
- *Strong analytical skills and sophisticated tools.*
- *Experience with big data and large-scale optimization engines:* Once all parameters have been defined, the handling of big data is the next challenge. The data used must be formatted appropriately. If it has gaps, companies need to close them with extrapolations or assumptions, in order to have a stable model.
- *An accurate, up-to-date, and costed Bill of Materials (BOM):* Core cost engineering is also about correctly allocating costs to components and functions, therefore an accurate and up-to-date BOM is important.
- *The right people who can follow the methodology correctly:* Core cost engineering takes diligence and people with experience in following processes.

Example: Low-Cost Airlines

Low-cost airlines disrupted the passenger flight segment by understanding that the core function that passengers want from a flight is to travel from A to B safely. Their interest in paying for legroom, newspapers, meals, luggage space, and drinks turned out to be limited. As a result, low-cost airlines made this optional and were able to decrease the overall cost of passenger air travel significantly.

Example: Shaving

Another example is the shaving equipment industry. It was dominated by Gillette over the past century. Gillette held about 70 percent of the market for traditional razor blades. Gillette spends money on marketing, packaging, and other overhead that drives up its cost. And buying a razor blade in a drugstore can be time consuming, since they are often locked up in a glass cabinet, and shoppers must get help from a clerk. Led by the Dollar Shave Club, several startups are challenging Gillette's dominant market position. They provide a convenient web-based order process and offer high-quality replenishment razor blades in plain packaging at a fraction of Gillette's price. Harry's, one of these startups, became vertically integrated after acquiring Feintechnik, a 95-year-old maker of high-end razor blades.

Example: Candles and Consumables – Focus on the Experience

A client that makes candles wanted to improve its EBIT. The company decided to begin with an analysis of the cost of production and the value of the item it was selling. By examining how the candles were made, sold and consumed, the company determined that the emotions attached to candles were important in the buying decision.

Together with Kearney, the company went through three further steps.

- *Step 1: Analyze how the product is made.* First the company found out through consumer sentiment analysis that the conventional myth of "more is better" no longer held true for its customers. It realized the product market had shifted from "give me a lot" to "give me something nice and different." It also began to understand that a certain kind of packaging actually did not stand for the brand, as the company had thought. Both insights led to rethinking the product. Why not create one that was differentiated to create more value, with packaging that cost less?
- *Step 2: Analyze how the product is sold.* Second, we challenged how the product was being sold as a wide assortment. The company studied how customers were buying lifestyle products: It was all about experience. Why not present the product in a studio/spa-like setting, where the product would be sold around themes. This would also help the store look fresh with every season.

> ━ *Step 3: Analyze how the product is consumed.* Lastly, consumers wanted variety associated with occasions and moods. Their desires had changed over the decades, but that had not yet been recognized by the candle maker. People wanted mood and occasion-specific products in their living rooms, which created the opportunity to reduce the amount of commodity sold and increase the frequency of small amounts sold. Meanwhile, the customer would enjoy the experience and the company would benefit from increased revenues.
>
> Using design to create value does not mean cheapening or reducing the product but creating an offering that customers care about and are willing to pay for.

A Brief History of Disruption

The world has seen many disruptions – especially in the past 100 years. Consider:
- *Disruption in the transportation and automotive sector:* Horse-drawn carriages were already used in Roman times, then disappeared and were rediscovered much later. The term was used as early as 1469. It was state-of-the-art for transportation for longer distances, but also within cities. In early March 1886, Gottlieb Daimler ordered a carriage at Wilhelm Wimpff in Stuttgart as a present for his wife, Emma. He then built an engine into the carriage – a real disruption.
- *Disruption in communication:* New communications technologies have always threatened to disrupt or actually done so. Think of the first fixed-line telephones. Now we have moved from there to mobile phones (for example Nokia), to smartphones with touchscreens (for example Apple and Samsung). Voice Over IP (VOIP) is another disruption – a technology that started with a lot of obstacles and poor quality but emerged over the years and replaced traditional phone lines.
- *Disruption in media:* Kodak used to be one of the worldwide leading companies for photo equipment – especially for analog film. The focus of the company was amateur photographers. This changed with digital photography, when the consumer was able to take an almost endless number of pictures without any additional cost.

What is interesting – yet a bit counterintuitive – in disruption?
- *Invention does not equal innovation, and innovation does not equal disruption.* When something disrupts the market and then gets enabled, it leads to the glory moments of achieving improvements, savings or growth. It is not a given that disruption always leads to success. Sometimes, the market is not ready for disruption, and certain innovations, and sometimes inventions, fail. It is important to differentiate between inventions and innovation. Invention is having an idea that is new and great, innovation means that this new and great idea is also successful on the market. At the same time, innovation is not always disruption. In many cases, founders of companies have great innovation, but are not disruptive. Think of the many tech companies that are evaluated as being disruptive, but most of them are just a bit more innovative than their competitors. Googles founders were doing things better than others, but not in a disruptive way.

- *Often, disruption is slow.* This is one sentence that many companies laugh at, if there is a discussion going on about disruption. It is counterintuitive, since disruption sounds like it must be fast, unexpected and probably even dangerous. Therefore, it is quite fascinating that some companies seem to be surprised when new trends and disruption arrive. Online music is such an example. It existed 20 years before it was seen as a disruptor in the industry and an "enemy" for CDs and DVDs. Usually, the impact and "danger" of disruptions are underestimated at the beginning. For example, the sales figures for CD producers did not fall significantly when digital music got established. On the flip side, after a certain period of time, the decline in the "conventional" market is much faster than expected; all in all, the impact is slower in the beginning and faster at the end. Another example is encyclopedias like the Brockhaus or Encyclopedia Britannica. At first, the companies did not take the competition of Wikipedia so seriously. The real impact took place 10 years after Wikipedia came to market in 2001. From these examples, we see that disruptors need some endurance and need to survive critical business phases at the beginning.

Procurement as a Disruptor

By asking the question – "How would a disruptor who is not burdened by legacy thinking or any other constraints do this?" – companies can open up the door to game-changing products or services. This approach requires a company to understand how suppliers create value for it and how it creates value for customers, so that it can apply new ideas. It also needs to be willing to set aside the conventions of the industry and be able to visualize how a product or service would be produced end to end. In the process, companies should focus on functions that really matter to customers, minimize life-cycle costs, eliminate non-value-adding components, design for manufacturing, configure an agile supply chain, and ensure high performance along the entire value chain.

What does it take to shake up the status quo in procurement?

- *Courage to challenge industry beliefs:* Disruption always means that there is a certain disconnect between the old and the new. Therefore, real disruptors challenge the common beliefs and rules of an industry by critically analyzing the beliefs in the industry, picking them apart, and showing how procurement can provide the basis for a new way to think about those beliefs.
- *Understanding of how a supplier is creating value:* To properly assess a supplier, companies need to have a deep understanding of the supplier's production and other processes. This requires cooperation from the supplier as well as an investment in time by the company which is doing the buying. In some cases, companies know the value that the supplier can create as well as or even better than the supplier itself, because of supplier immaturity and a wider understanding of the value chain.
- *Understanding of how the company creates value for its customers:* Without the customer in mind, companies can hardly anticipate needs and wants. The second axis of the Disruptive Procurement framework is exactly this: the understanding of the value for the customer. Surprisingly, only few companies really know this dimension, and even fewer know both dimensions.

4

— *Open mindedness, creativity and innovation capabilities:* Procurement as a disruptor requires seeing things differently than all the rest. This involves open mindedness and creativity, backed by investment and capabilities focused on innovation. Companies that are not open and curious will never become disruptors.

— *CEO and/or founder backing:* For procurement to shake up the system, the top management of a company must be on board. A radical disruptor will not always be loved among incumbent suppliers and industry organizations. Therefore, procurement departments that aim to disrupt need to cover their backs and have top management behind them as they chart a new course. Most examples show us that disruptive products and services become successful over time when top management is fully behind the idea and can eliminate hurdles. The CEO or founder can enable cross-functional collaboration, invest the right amount of money, and help align procurement with the company's strategy.

— *Strong communication skills on all levels.*

Example: Tesla and Disruption in the Automotive Industry

Even though the automotive industry is a leader in procurement, the industry has gotten complacent at times. Consider Tesla.

Elon Musk, the founder of Tesla, released the model S, which was a shock to the automotive industry. Everybody expected the car to perform poorly in crash tests and in handling, but the opposite was true, since there is no engine under the hood that can be pushed toward the passenger in frontal crashes. The car performed better than comparable large vehicles from Audi, BMW and Mercedes. Similarly, heavy batteries in Tesla's sandwich floor make it drive more like a Ferrari than a four-door sedan.

Even more worrying for traditional carmakers than the surprisingly good performance of Tesla cars was their electronic architecture. Tesla's model S has been dubbed a smartphone on wheels, and essentially it is. The majority of Tesla's employees have a background in high-tech consumer electronics, and it shows in the car. Other cars have arrays of switches and dials, while the model S has one large touch screen. Every Tesla is continuously online and receives software updates.

The consumer electronics industry teaches people to deal with technology cycles of a year or less. Compare this to the automotive industry's typical multi-year technology cycles. In automotive, products get frozen in the past.

At Tesla, procurement focused on completely different components than an established car manufacturer would focus on. Electricity management and electrical components were the focus, compared to fuel engines and steel. Tesla disrupted the market, and now we see the market adopting many ideas from Tesla.

Example: Aluminum Buying and Changing the Rules of the Game

Here's another example of disruption that is not a newly invented or designed product, and it's not digital. It is a breakthrough in the buying of aluminum as a raw material.

A leading automotive OEM began to consider how to buy aluminum without being influenced by swings in prices from market hedges, speculation and financial instruments. Usually, the London Metal Exchange (LME) was the source of current prices and for futures. But what would happen if the constraint of finding the "right" price on the LME was not there? This OEM worked with consultants to understand every detail of supply, demand, input factors and cost.

The company built a pricing model to analyze prices for aluminum over 20 years. It found that the average price of aluminum was more or less the production cost with an appropriate margin. So, the company challenged the market belief that stable pricing contracts could not be in place.

At first the OEM did not even find one supplier that was willing to discuss this simple yet disruptive approach. Eventually, it found one in the Middle East that had invested significantly in its own capacity and was looking for stable orders rather than maximizing profits. The two companies agreed on stable pricing, and the contract remains unique in the market.

Getting Started with Disruptive Procurement

Looking at these nine building blocks as a whole, we realize that many companies find themselves squarely in the lower left-hand area – for example in the desktop procurement box, while the goal is to move toward the top right (see ◘ Fig. 4.1).

To turn this around, start by using the framework to chart the future trajectory of your procurement function.

Clarify your ambition for the product or service line in scope. Do we want it to become a disruptor? Do we have the management capacity, the cross functional buy-in, and the shareholder mandate to do that?

For many companies, pushing toward a supplier fitness program or design for value creation may be a reasonable way forward.

For each division, region, product or service line in your company, you may chart a different trajectory.

What's important is to adopt a beginner's mindset, spend far more time with suppliers and customers, and interact more often with internal stakeholders (maybe with a coffee in one hand and a screwdriver in the other).

4

PERL – Product Excellence and Renewal Labs

Kearney – together with a global ecosystem of partners from design-thinking experts to software and product engineers – provides clients with a structured way to think more holistically about product and service design, to innovate and to look for cost savings. We call this our Product Excellence and Renewal Labs approach, or a PERLab approach for short.

Goals of PERL

The main objective of PERL is to achieve design-driven EBIT improvements of products and services that will impact the bottom and top lines. This comes with improved product designs – which starts with understanding what customers care about, not want or need. If companies focus on wants, they won't innovate; if they focus on needs, they create commodities.

The next step is to understand what constitutes a product by conducting product teardowns, as well as competitor product teardowns. Both help us understand how a product was designed and constructed, and this lays the foundation for ideas for reducing costs and improving sales. It's also a starting point for exploring new business models. Rigorous groundwork comes together in design workshops where we challenge every idea, sub-system, component and material to make sure any idea that passes our "filter" is sound. Finally, we develop the business cases and roadmaps to put the ideas into action.

Why Is PERL Necessary?

Analysis shows that companies with design and product architecture at their center have outperformed the S&P 500 over the last 10 years by more than 200 percent. Many corporations now have internal design, product composition and product architecture functions, but often, those functions get bogged down with day-to-day operations and are not producing new prototypes.

Ask any design engineer: There is never enough time to sit back and look at the design from every angle. There is always pressure to get to market, which leads to sub-optimal decisions. Beyond that, most organizational functions work too independently from one another – marketing, product development and procurement rarely work in concert.

Early-stage engagement can maximize end-to-end control over product life-cycle value and costs (see ◘ Fig. 4.4). Many experts say that 70 percent of the cost of a product or service is determined in the idea and concept phase. Indeed, companies can make a big impact on costs by (1) challenging industry beliefs, (2) redefining specifications (3) designing to assembly and efficient manufacturing (4) optimizing value chain design and (5) incorporating the latest technologies.

But PERL is not only something for early engagement. It can also help overcome shortcomings throughout the whole product lifecycle (see ◘ Fig. 4.5). PERL includes most elements needed for Disruptive Procurement. In fact, it is an enabler for it. It addresses these questions:

- *Design:* Can products be designed to reduce complexity or the number of parts? How can we conceptualize design alternatives? Can we learn from different industries?

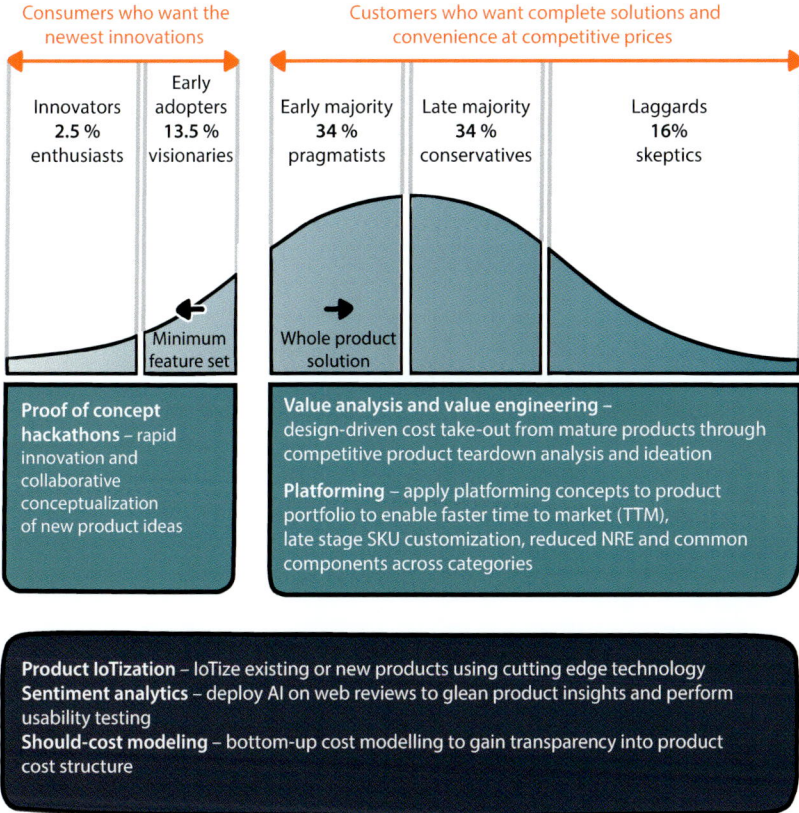

Consumers who want the newest innovations

Customers who want complete solutions and convenience at competitive prices

| Innovators 2.5% enthusiasts | Early adopters 13.5% visionaries | Early majority 34% pragmatists | Late majority 34% conservatives | Laggards 16% skeptics |

Minimum feature set

Whole product solution

Proof of concept hackathons – rapid innovation and collaborative conceptualization of new product ideas

Value analysis and value engineering – design-driven cost take-out from mature products through competitive product teardown analysis and ideation

Platforming – apply platforming concepts to product portfolio to enable faster time to market (TTM), late stage SKU customization, reduced NRE and common components across categories

Product IoTization – IoTize existing or new products using cutting edge technology
Sentiment analytics – deploy AI on web reviews to glean product insights and perform usability testing
Should-cost modeling – bottom-up cost modelling to gain transparency into product cost structure

▢ Fig. 4.4 PERLab – designing value throughout the product lifecycle

— *Processes:* Which manufacturing processes are used in making the product? Can we substitute alternative processes to increase throughput and/or increase value?
— *Features:* What do customer's value? How do these features compare to those of competitors at different price points? How is each feature implemented, and what is the associated cost?
— *Materials:* Which substitutes are available? What is the impact of using alternative materials (utility, quality, look and feel)? Can we use off-the shelf parts vs. custom designed parts?

By addressing these questions, companies can begin to drive down the overall cost and increase value (see ▢ Fig. 4.6).

How Do You Quickly Increase the Enterprise Value of a Company?
PERL helped uncover a cost reduction opportunity of more than 50 percent for a lifestyle and healthcare startup. About 30 percent of the savings were realized within the first 12 months; the rest were designed into the next generation of

4

VOICE OF CONSUMER

- Review of user / consumer value drivers based on internal research and voice of customers
- Sentiment analysis conducted using machine-learning (Natural Language Processing) based methodology / tools

PRODUCT TEARDOWNS

- Teardowns of client and competitor products (comparable, as well as good, better, best level)
- Link between product components and user / consumer value drivers

BOM AND BOP ANALYSIS

- Analysis of Bill of Materials with catalog components to identify cost drivers
- Bill of Process consisting of equipment use, assembling and machining time to identify process-driven cost drivers

IDEATION & DESIGN WORKSHOP

- Cross-functional collaboration and brainstorming of ideas captured, based on design, process and material changes
- End stage product visualization from partnership with industrial designers

PRIORITIZED IMPLEMEN-TATION PLAN

- Sizing of ideas along with feasibility assessment
- Documentation of ideas and teardown findings into funnel for VAVE implementation
- Portfolio rationalization and market assessment for whitespace opportunities to be targeted

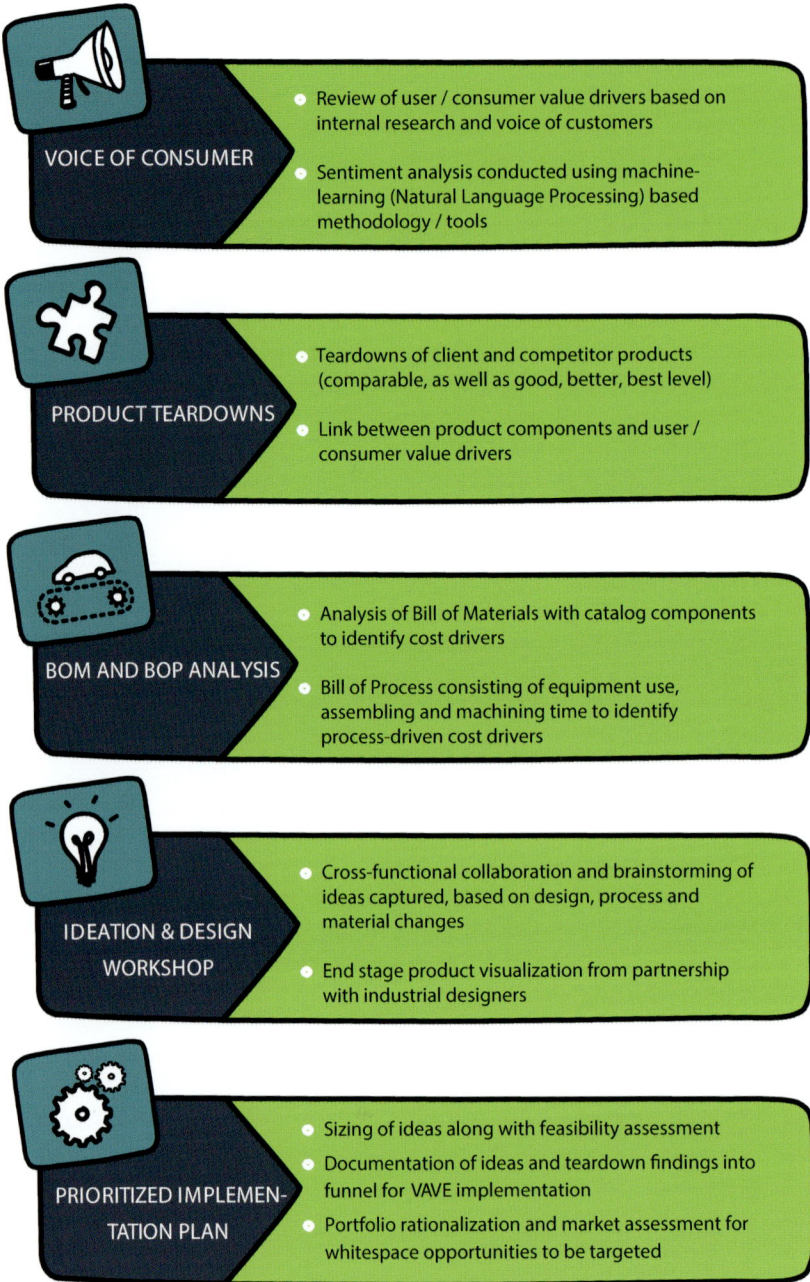

■ **Fig. 4.5**   PERL approach for end-to-end implications of design-driven decisions

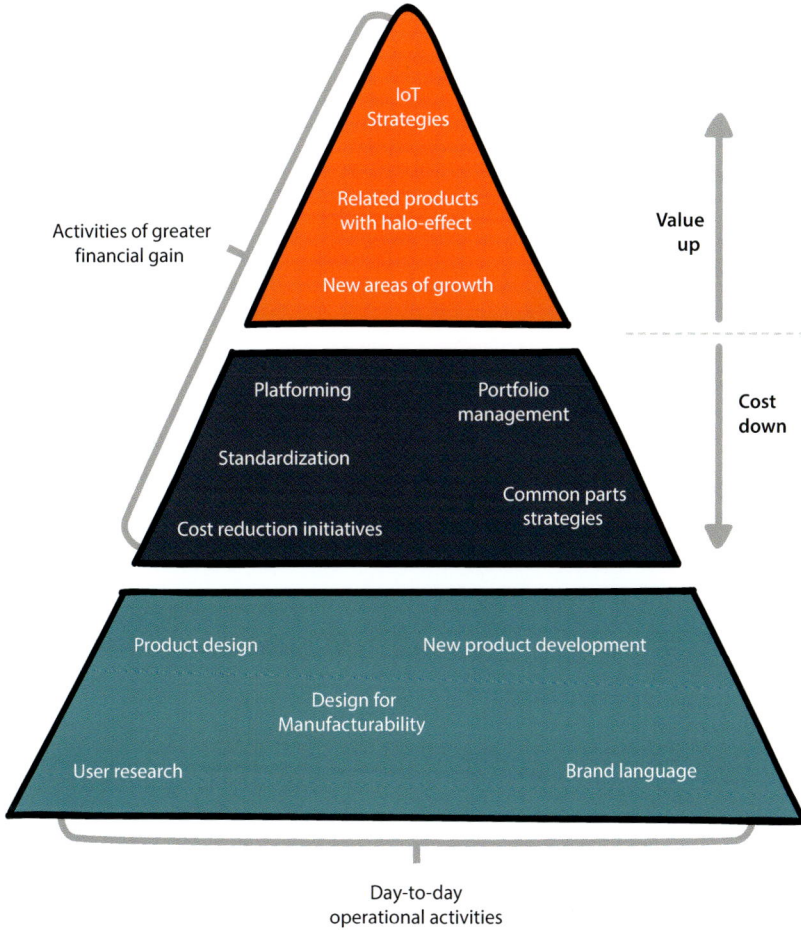

☐ Fig. 4.6 Value optimization with PERLab

products and services. As a result, the company, which was growing fast, saw its enterprise value rise because of its EBIT improvement.

The startup faced the same problem as many others: Its costs were too high as it raced to market, and that caused major hurdles. The PERL approach helped the company make its product ruthlessly competitive and improve customer experience.

To begin with, the PERL approach requires studying the company's products, as well as products from competitors, to understand:

– What do customers care about?
– What drives cost?

— What are the constraints for design, and what are some self-imposed constraints?
— What are the procurement practices of the company?
— Can the supply base rigorously reduce costs and improve quality?

The result: With PERL, the company was able to identify improvements in cost of goods and services through a series of activities over six weeks. The client leadership was part of every single activity so that there was no need to spend time getting stakeholder buy-in. The buy-in happened at every step of way.

Example: PERL and a Scientific and Medical Equipment OEM
The PERL approach helped reduce the cost of a medical and scientific product by more than 75 percent by challenging the entire premise behind the product design and breaking down the product into its fundamental functions.
An initial analysis revealed:
— The product was very well respected in the industry but at the same time the company had a less-than-optimal ability to deliver current-generation electronics and software
— Most of the logic in the product was still electronics-based instead of software-based
— The electronics design was at least two to three generations old, leading to massive supply continuity risk, as several components became obsolete
— The product had no ability to scale – adding Internet of Things capabilities would be very complex, as integration with the old design would require the creation of integration layers that added no value

As part of the PERL process, the client asked itself: "Does it have to be done this way, or are there alternatives to this design?" Using both internal and open-sourced ideas, we designed a working prototype in four weeks at less than 75 percent of the cost of the product we started off with. Of course, the technologies we used were not available when the original product was designed. Until this time, no one ever thought of disrupting their own technology.
What started as a cost reduction program resulted in by-products that far outweighed the cost-reduction benefits. These include:
— A systems integration approach to product design that used off-the-shelf electronics
— Future-proofing the product – the standard computing boards allow plug-and-play replacements
— Enhanced features, such as moving to the latest electronics that enable IoT and connectivity as a byproduct

Example: Industrial Goods

PERLab was asked to bring design thinking to the industrial goods world and achieve significant cost reductions and a value increase for a leading European machinery manufacturer.

The client was a global market leader in technology for metal forming machines, tools and processing. Traditionally, every machine was developed independently and tailored to specific requirements, giving the company a reputation for quality.

However, the company was coming under pressure from other players that offered more attractive pricing and differentiation in product design. The company wanted to reduce production costs by more than 20 percent while increasing the perception of quality and brand by the customers. It put the project focus on jointly developing machine enclosures. As part of the overhaul, all visible and safety-relevant parts of the enclosures were newly designed, which helped give a consistent image of high quality.

At the same time, the company reduced the number of different parts to a minimum by combining standardized components for each specific machine. This helped to drastically reduce costs for tooling, manufacturing, inventory and logistics.

Overall, the platforming strategy achieved the three main objectives:

- Enclosures could be developed using standardized building blocks which significantly reduced the time to market and development effort
- The principle of parts commonality led to significant savings in procurement and logistics
- Brand and quality perception increased significantly through more sophisticated design and material selection

Implementing a Platform Strategy in Material Handling Equipment

With the PERLab approach, a global leader in material handling equipment introduced a platform that reduced complexity and cost, while retaining the ability to offer tailored solutions and a variety of products for customers.

Together with stakeholders from marketing, R&D, procurement and production, we followed a design-focused approach to jointly develop the concept. We studied the real requirements of the company's end users and observed their behaviors, identifying which features were truly relevant.

In the end, the company built a fully functional prototype to validate the design and prove feasibility, and the platform strategy resulted in reduced costs and increased value for customers. This was achieved through:

- Cost reductions and harmonization in procurement, production and supply chain
- Reduced time-to-market for new products through flexible design
- Low marginal cost of customization to meet customer needs

Procurement Frameworks

Earlier we discussed the Purchasing Chessboard®, which focuses on categories and optimizing those categories. It's important to note that the path to Disruptive Procurement requires a different view than using the Purchasing Chessboard® framework: Namely, to become a disruptor in procurement, companies must focus on the end product or service and how it brings value to the customer.

In addition, the objective of Disruptive Procurement distinguishes it from other frameworks (see ◘ Fig. 4.7). In Disruptive Procurement, the goal is to do things completely different within an industry by challenging industry beliefs and rethinking products and services. Finally, Disruptive Procurement is best mandated by the CEO, whereas other approaches can be bottom-up or cross-functional.

	The purchasing chessboard®	True srm	Procurement as a disruptor	Holistic procurement transformation
Focus	Category	Supplier	Entire product or service lines	Organization
Objective	Achieve the highest possible sustainable savings and generate value	Obtain competitive advantage and maximize value generated with suppliers	Reinvent the way things are done within an industry	Transform the organization, balance hard and soft facts, create internal and external effectiveness
How the framework is deployed	Apply one or a combination of the 64 levers based on a specific balance of supply and demand	Apply tailored interaction models based on performance and strategic potential; Requires broad cross-functional alignment	Leverage deep knowledge on value creation process at the supplier as well as each company's own value creation process; Best mandated by the CEO because it leaves no paradigm unchallenged when fully deployed	Based on board mandate to transform the organization

◘ **Fig. 4.7**   Procurement frameworks: Focus, objective, deployment methods

Outlook

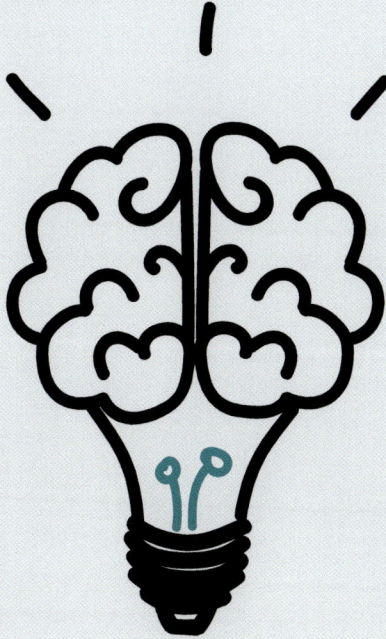

Contents

© Springer Nature Switzerland AG 2020
M. F. Strohmer et al., *Disruptive Procurement*, https://doi.org/10.1007/978-3-030-38950-5_5

Procurement Is Becoming Smaller, Smarter and Speedier

Looking ahead at the future of procurement, we believe companies must prepare now for a vastly different operating environment and a completely new role for the function. If the transition is managed right, procurement will emerge as a true strategic partner for the business, using its immense data resources and analytics to guide the business and anticipate and manage risk.

We predict that "pure" operational procurement will first be outsourced and then fully automated by 2035, which is the basis for procurement's transformation. In other words, few or no people will be employed in operational procurement by then. Systems will operate processes independently within a small margin of error, and they will do so on a continuous basis. For instance, requisitions will be done automatically, based on machine and warehouse data sent via sensors. No manual work will be necessary. Instead, highly skilled professionals will be needed for procurement strategy and analytics, as well as for overseeing the machines that are handling operational procurement processes.

Megatrends and global shifts are driving these changes. They are causing supply chains to be restructured and even more to be demanded from supply management. For instance, the recent rise of populism and greater focus on sustainability are forcing companies to rethink their bias toward globalism, while digital technologies are reshaping processes, changing business models and impacting cost structures. Companies have to consider their costs because of profitability. But in the future, cost considerations will be counter-balanced by concerns about sustainability across the entire value chain.

In this new evolution, procurement professionals will no longer be seen as just bargain-hunters and contract negotiators. Instead, procurement will be a major source of the latest challenges to industry beliefs.

These trends accelerate the need for CPOs to manage change and deliver competitive advantage from the supply management component of their value chain. To this end, we have identified trends to watch in procurement and formulated recommendations for a response to the fundamental changes taking place.

Trend 1: Larger and More Complex Value Chain Processes

First, we expect in the years to come that your company will have to manage *larger and more complex value chain processes* than now. This means more steps in the value chain, more participants (for example, second and third-level supply partners), more data, more interfaces between the IT system and the organization, more processes, as well as more possibilities for innovation and savings.

Here we want to emphasize that it is not only the value chain itself that will be more difficult to manage because of its greater scope and scale, but also the related processes for procurement.

Procurement processes will be more unwieldy, involve more partners and be the source of more surprises than in the past, making them increasingly difficult to manage and to harmonize.

Some of the new complexity comes from a move to multi-localism by companies that in the past had invested in global, harmonized and unified supply chains.

These companies have left behind their focus on growth through economies of scale, efficiency enhancements, and the sale of mass-market products. Instead, they are responding to the needs and preferences of local communities. This requires a fundamental shift in the structure of supply chains and adds complexity to business operations because of customizations for local preferences.

The additional complexity also comes through new roles for procurement.

If procurement will be a driver of innovation along with its work in product-cost optimization, it must be a party in actively managing the entire value chain for a company, including in R&D. It is also ideally positioned to bring all parties along the value chain together to solve problems, for instance problems with material quality. Often, material problems cannot be traced back to a single supplier. Playing a blame game, or allowing one to be played, doesn't help. Procurement can help by bringing in an objective third party.

In the end, external spend represents 50–60 percent of the budget of most companies. As procurement becomes more digital and strategic, it will be capable of and should exercise even more control over external spending. As a result, we believe procurement should also have 50 to 60 percent of the say in companies.

Trend 2: Procurement as the Central Data Analytics Hub

Second, we believe the journey to procurement excellence through digital tools has only begun, and there's much to be discovered, mined and excavated about your own business, your suppliers and the categories in which you procure.

Procurement is a profoundly data-drive discipline, giving it high potential for improvement through new tools like artificial intelligence (AI) and other advanced analytics. This means there's much room for creativity with each new tool that is introduced or data set that can be created or added to a model.

But many in the enterprise – and in procurement – have not yet internalized this change in identity for the function. They still see procurement as "the ones in charge of reducing costs for products or services," instead of the "the ones with the best ideas based on sound data analysis."

The link between procurement and analytics is a logical one because so much data comes together in procurement, such as demand and pricing data, and data on a product's feasibility, quality and technical specifications. In general, we have seen an "explosion" in the richness and variety of data that can be analyzed. To conduct sophisticated analyses, procurement must combine this rich data with its understanding of what impacts price most, such as transportation costs, warehousing costs, or product quality or material. In most cases, companies use very little of the data they could theoretically use when procuring a product. We expect more data sharing with all value chain partners and regular analysis of data generated by the smart factory applications in one's own company – and that of suppliers.

Tool selection and implementation are critical for improved efficiency and effectiveness from procurement. Some standards are emerging in the industry for tools on spend transparency, including visualization. Tools must be adapted or created for emerging categories. In many cases, the categories themselves are heavily data driven, such as procuring solutions for digital marketing. Here prices for solutions may be linked to the amount of thousand impressions. Another example is procuring custom software development. Here baseline or benchmark prices may be hard to determine.

Trend 3: Procurement as a Service-Oriented Innovation Scout

In the past, procurement was only brought into the innovation process after suppliers were involved by R&D directly. Going forward, procurement must be involved much earlier in the product and service design process to make use of its unique ability to scout innovation in the market and from partners. Procurement should become a trusted partner for extracting value from the supply chain from an operational perspective, through cost savings on products and services, and by identifying, inspiring, motivating and enabling suppliers to bring forth innovation and do it in a socially-responsible way.

In our vision for companies, up to 80 percent of the company's own value will be influenced by suppliers, and partnerships will generate up to 90 percent of innovations. This puts a great responsibility on procurement to help identify and secure the right partners. From a sustainability point of view, that may also mean ensuring suppliers' processes conform to the company's own code of conduct, such as guidelines on the use of natural resources. Sometimes companies will conclude that it is better to pay more for a product or component which is manufactured according to sustainability standards, such as those for using recycled elements.

In solid partnerships with the right legal basis that allows partners to share ideas, all value chain partners should be checking in with each other regularly to discuss their innovation efforts. Each party should talk about how it can be of service to the network and which benefits it is looking for from it. With each success achieved within the value chain, common experience, trust and loyalty grow. If some suppliers are not contributing, it may be time to think about how to modify their roles or replace them entirely.

If the collaboration between procurement and other company divisions, such as R&D and sales, is structured properly, procurement can be a major help in shortening product development cycles with its understanding of both markets and technology and by lowering production costs through design. For instance, with its overview of what suppliers are working on, procurement may have ideas about how to commoditize all those areas of a product or service that have little or no contact with the customer – for example, things that are in the box or behind the screen.

Sometimes that structure will involve shared responsibility with shared KPIs; other times, those creating new products and services can be given a dedicated person in procurement who is tasked with providing support.

Procurement must be like a mind-reader: It must deliver those items that marketing and sales need in the future (as well as now). For example, decades ago, airlines sought high-margin products they could sell to their captive audiences on planes and began to offer duty-free cosmetics, cigarettes and liquor, as well as high-priced snacks. Similarly in the future, it will be procurement's job to find the items with the right margins and features that can be cross-sold to customers. The integration of IT systems from sales and R&D with that of procurement will help. The system will know what R&D is planning and make pre-emptive suggestions about suitable products based on the criteria inputted, providing the full details about price and features and what can be customized.

How to Boost Procurement

Given the larger and more complex value chain processes procurement will need to manage in the future, and the changing role of procurement into specialists in data science and innovation scouting, we see three actions companies can and should take now: skill up the procurement workforce, make "faster" a priority, and lay the digital groundwork for completely automated operational procurement.

What to Do #1: Skill up the Procurement Staff

Companies must properly manage the transition from running operational procurement departments with a large number of full-time employees to operating a highly-skilled, strategic procurement department (see ◘ Fig. 5.1). Procurement must start now to help its workforce skill up and build the capabilities it needs to fill its new roles. This includes skills related to digital technologies and managing the interface across functions. Procurement professionals also need to manage complex projects and be able to think strategically. We should also remember that operational procurement processes have to be maintained, improved, monitored and changed for new products, and interfaces have to be managed in parallel because of new IT systems or tools.

In the end, procurement professionals need to fit into two distinct profiles: The first is those who are the networkers with high emotional intelligence and capable of being a catalyst for the whole company. These are the people who must motivate and facilitate suppliers to bring in innovation, and they must do so hand in hand with people from other divisions across the company.

The second profile is more technical. Procurement also needs data scientists with strong analytic skills. These professionals must be able to identify new sources of data and then wrangle the data to make it usable. From there, procurement should make recommendations for concrete actions based on knowledge gleaned

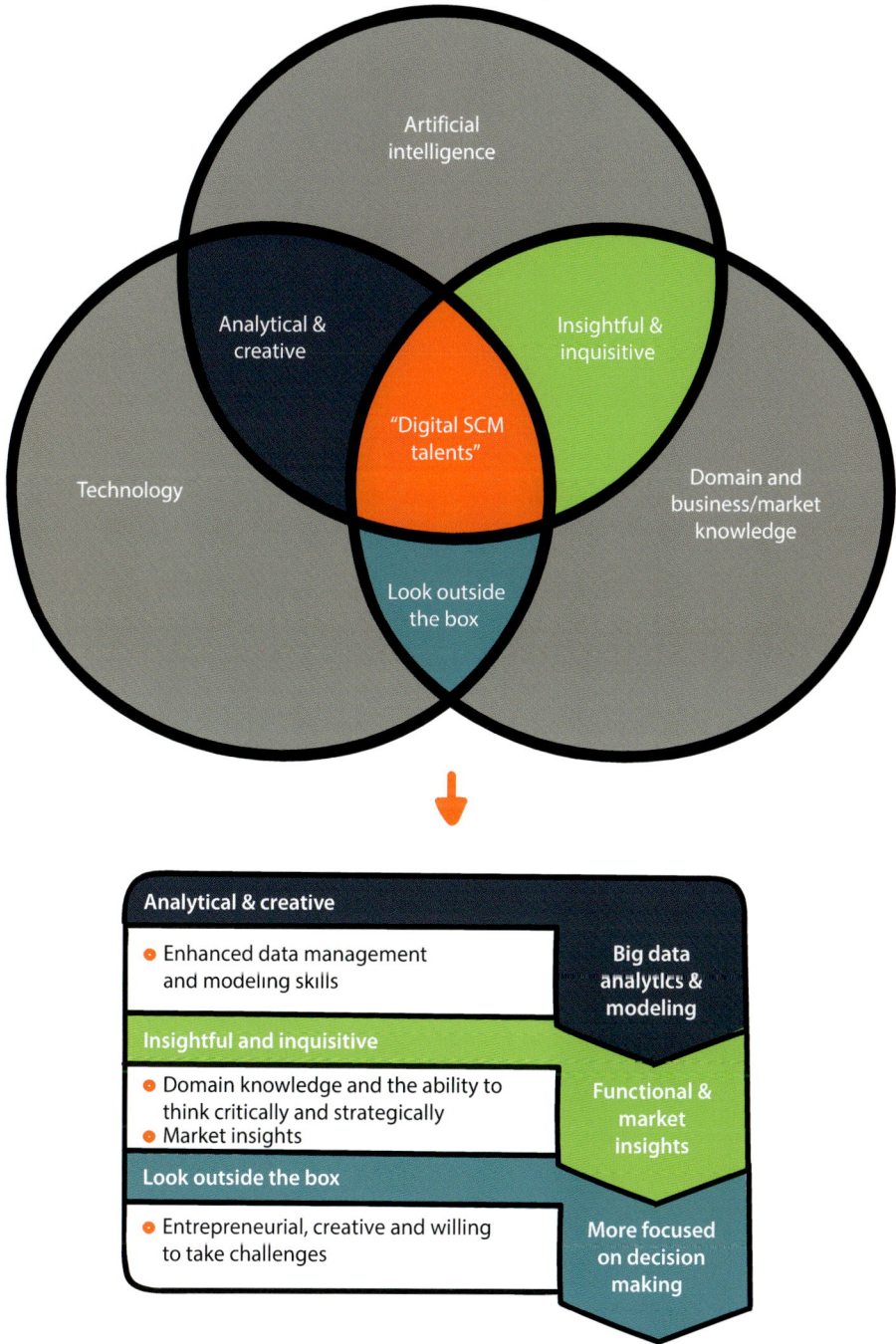

Fig. 5.1 Talent needs for future supply chains

from the data. Furthermore, procurement needs specialists who can interface with IT, for instance when a new algorithm is being developed and specialized knowledge about both IT and procurement are needed. Technical procurement professionals will also need a deep understanding of the AI that enables complex planning methodologies, such as those based on game theory.

Working together, procurement professionals with both technical and softer skills must be able to quickly visualize how changes for the supplier of a supplier of a supplier will impact their own company. For example, when the nuclear accident happened in Fukushima in 2011, automakers saw that their reliance on a single supplier of a pigment to make car paint shine led to production difficulties. Knowing these type of details and being able to act on them fast are crucial and will be more so in the future.

As procurement staff skill up and regularly help in scenario planning and the creation of digital twins for products and processes, it will gain power and respect within the organization, based on its unique ability to visualize the impact of changes way down the line. This type of thinking and preparation will also help procurement do its job faster during a real emergency or competitive challenge, which is essential in today's market and brings us to our next point.

What to Do #2: Think Speed

For procurement to operate at its full potential, it must get faster at gathering and understanding information about the value chain, the players and the industry trends of diverse suppliers. But the reality is that few value-chain partners share data on a regular basis because of technical data integration problems, supplier unwillingness or insecurity about sharing.

Companies need to act quickly to overcome these hurdles to capture the potential.

New analytics capabilities applied to real-time or close to real-time data will make it possible for procurement to work faster. Procurement can set up processes that provide a real-time, big picture overview and allow for ever-more sources of data to be included in an orderly fashion.

Already, Optical Character Recognition (OCR) technology can extract text from invoices, contracts and other documents and convert it to a readable format. Combined with AI, OCR technologies can harvest and analyze vast amounts of new data at incredible speeds.

Being fast helps in negotiations, too. Today, procurement professionals may still negotiate without knowing the price history and price expectations for input materials. An example would be a procurement professional negotiating over plastic packaging prices without having understood price developments for resin. Apps are available that provide negotiators with relevant, real-time price data of product inputs that can be used during negotiations. Such tools should be a staple in procurement departments.

Finally, procurement can get faster with better organizational setups, such as those that enable working in sprints to develop solutions and analyze particular data. We expect that procurement will work, at least partly, as pools of buyers, rather than dedicated buyers per category.

Of course, the changes made must be in line with the overall procurement strategy. Kearney research has shown that lack of budget is what holds most companies back in their digital procurement, making prioritized rollouts that much more important.

As we have said, procurement is getting smaller and smarter. But if it remains slow, how can leanness and brains help against competitors who pounce faster? There's only one way to move forward: Procurement must become smaller, smarter *and* speedier. It's foreseeable that procurement may one day be measured on time-to-market.

Indeed, we expect the gaps between leading companies and followers to increase as the push for digitalization continues. And those companies that have more data and a smarter approach to quickly extracting knowledge from it will have a distinct advantage.

What to Do #3: Lay the Digital Groundwork Now

In this book, we have mapped out a path forward for procurement to become a strong partner for delivering strategic value to the business. It is based on the assumption that companies do not lose a minute on laying the digital groundwork, as discussed in ► Chapter 3.

The starting point is procurement having its own digital agenda and a strong focus on the digital tools that will help it work more effectively, not just efficiently. Then procurement will be able to provide strategic advice to the business and present its own ideas for innovation, social responsibility and optimization.

This will happen with a full set of tools that enable a clear view of the entire value chain and make it possible to do wide-ranging custom analyses to prove a point about the business or the validity of a new idea. The same digital tools will also put procurement on the front lines for managing risk for the entire company.

That said, the procurement function cannot become a disruptor, as discussed in ► Chapter 4, if the basic building blocks of desktop procurement, such as a supplier fitness program or core cost engineering, are not implemented and digitized. This is the groundwork on which procurement itself can become disruptive, for instance by collecting data about all negotiations done in the past by a company and analyzing it for trends and understanding that can help in current negotiations.

We cannot stress it more: Do not allow a train wreck to happen in your organization by failing to digitize the basic processes which can be made digital today in an economical way. Do not wait until the last moment and expect to implement advanced tools, if the foundational work of making operational procurement digital is not yet done.

In the end, the defining difference between leaders and laggards will be how they use digital tools for procurement – for example their creativity in collecting and combining data sources, and which strategies they pursue based on that data and the various capabilities they have acquired.

What's Next

The days of creating easy savings by pressuring or changing suppliers are gone. Optimizing products together, in partnership with suppliers, will be more effective than pushing for suppliers to do it a certain way. If you want your procurement function to remain viable, you must stay abreast of or out in front of the trends and respond to them accordingly. Much of that response may involve implementing advanced analytics, after creating a solid foundation of excellence in established procurement processes, for instance with 360° supplier development. Otherwise, your procurement function will become obsolete.

Considering all the changes needed for procurement to reach its full potential as a data-driven source of insight, it's important to remember that the overall cost of running a top-notch procurement organization will not decrease. Although savings will be reached through process automation of operational tasks, procurement needs more skilled and qualified people and more IT support, which will cut into cost savings.

As operational procurement processes become automated, we believe the procurement function can take on more strategic roles to create value for the company, sharing its unique knowledge about opportunities and risks.

And whether the procurement function still exists in 2050, well, that remains to be seen.